NEW DIRECTIONS FOR TEACHING AND LEARNING

Robert J. Menges, *Northwestern University*
EDITOR-IN-CHIEF

Marilla D. Svinicki, *University of Texas, Austin*
ASSOCIATE EDITOR

The Impact of Technology on Faculty Development, Life, and Work

Kay Herr Gillespie
University of Georgia

EDITOR

Number 76, Winter 1998

JOSSEY-BASS PUBLISHERS
San Francisco

LB
1028.3
.I55
1998

THE IMPACT OF TECHNOLOGY ON FACULTY DEVELOPMENT, LIFE, AND WORK
Kay Herr Gillespie (ed.)
New Directions for Teaching and Learning, no. 76
Robert J. Menges, Editor-in-Chief
Marilla D. Svinicki, Associate Editor

Copyright © 1998 Jossey-Bass Inc., Publishers, 350 Sansome Street, San Francisco, CA 94104.

All rights reserved. No part of this publication may be reproduced, stored in a retrieval system, or transmitted, in any form or by any means, electronic, mechanical, photocopying, recording, or otherwise, without the prior written permission of the publisher.

Microfilm copies of issues and articles are available in 16mm and 35mm, as well as microfiche in 105mm, through University Microfilms Inc., 300 North Zeeb Road, Ann Arbor, Michigan 48106-1346.

ISSN 0271-0633   ISBN 0-7879-4280-4

NEW DIRECTIONS FOR TEACHING AND LEARNING is part of The Jossey-Bass Higher and Adult Education Series and is published quarterly by Jossey-Bass Inc., Publishers, 350 Sansome Street, San Francisco, California 94104-1342. Periodicals postage paid at San Francisco, California, and at additional mailing offices. Postmaster: Send address changes to New Directions for Teaching and Learning, Jossey-Bass Inc., Publishers, 350 Sansome Street, San Francisco, California 94104-1342.

New Directions for Teaching and Learning is indexed in College Student Personnel Abstracts, Contents Pages in Education, and Current Index to Journals in Education (ERIC).

SUBSCRIPTIONS cost $56.00 for individuals and $99.00 for institutions, agencies, and libraries. Prices subject to change.

EDITORIAL CORRESPONDENCE should be sent to the associate editor, Marilla D. Svinicki, The Center for Teaching Effectiveness, University of Texas at Austin, Main Building 2200, Austin, TX 78712-1111.

Cover photograph by Richard Blair/Color & Light © 1990.

www.josseybass.com

Printed in the United States of America on acid-free recycled paper containing 100 percent recovered waste paper, of which at least 20 percent is postconsumer waste.

WIDENER UNIVERSITY
WOLFGRAM
LIBRARY
CHESTER, PA

Contents

FROM THE SERIES EDITORS

About This Publication. Since 1980, *New Directions for Teaching and Learning (NDTL)* has brought a unique blend of theory, research, and practice to leaders in postsecondary education. *NDTL* sourcebooks strive not only for solid substance but also for timeliness, compactness, and accessibility.

The series has four goals: to inform readers about current and future directions in teaching and learning in postsecondary education, to illuminate the context that shapes these new directions, to illustrate these new directions through examples from real settings, and to propose ways in which these new directions can be incorporated into still other settings.

This publication reflects our view that teaching deserves respect as a high form of scholarship. We believe that significant scholarship is conducted not only by researchers who report results of empirical investigations but also by practitioners who share disciplined reflections about teaching. Contributors to *NDTL* approach questions of teaching and learning as seriously as they approach substantive questions in their own disciplines, and they deal not only with pedagogical issues but also with the intellectual and social context in which these issues arise. Authors deal on the one hand with theory and research and on the other with practice, and they translate from research and theory to practice and back again.

About This Volume. In this volume the authors are taking the issue of technology in higher education to a new level of analysis. Instead of concentrating only on the reform that technology offers teaching, these authors explore the many ways that technology can affect the multiple facets of faculty life and work. Their insights bring a fresh perspective on what seems to be an all-important topic for higher education now and in the future.

Robert J. Menges, *Editor-in-Chief*
Marilla D. Svinicki, *Associate Editor*

Editor's Notes

A critical and global issue in higher education today is the implementation of technology in our individual, institutional, and collective settings for the enhancement of teaching and learning in the widest sense. The scope of the issue we face is inclusive not only of undergraduate and graduate teaching and learning within the classroom and beyond, but also of the research and service or outreach components of our mission—in short, everything we do in higher education.

In this sourcebook we explore significant issues relating to the impact of technology on faculty development, life, and work; and we do so with a foundation of assumptions. These are (1) that these four areas are inextricably tied together—technology, faculty members' lives and work, and faculty development; (2) that learning by doing is effective learning; (3) that the rapidity of technological change and its importance for all of education, not just higher education, will neither diminish nor disappear; and (4) that it is imperative for us to reflect and then to act in increasingly vigorous ways on the possibilities and realities of technological change. We can do so positively and with enthusiasm about improving the quality of all that we have been seeking to do for centuries—structuring ever more effectively the formalized education and subsequent enlightenment of those who come after us, and of ourselves in the process.

Readers are probably not likely to wonder about the meaning of *faculty life and work* for this volume. There may, however, be those who ask what we mean by *faculty development.* Definitions of the term abound; and we commonly speak of additional categories such as instructional, organizational, administrative, and personal development as well as the umbrella term of professional development. For the purposes of this volume we opt for a very simple definition to undergird our discussions: faculty development is a purposeful, institutionalized approach to doing that which helps faculty members do their work better as individuals within an institution and within the collective enterprise of higher education. Beyond such long institutionalized practices as sabbaticals and travel and research grants, the structures of faculty development, as it has developed since the 1960s, are seminars, workshops, discussion groups in varying formats, and individual consultation—all of this not necessarily restricted to matters of teaching and learning.

As we seek to deal with the degree of overwhelming possibilities of change swirling around us, however, it is enlightening to return to earlier thought about faculty development, which enriches our reflections. For example, twenty-five years ago Martin Freedman (1973) edited the very first volume of the Jossey-Bass series New Directions for Higher Education, and it was entitled *Facilitating Faculty Development.* In the "Editor's Notes" he wrote, "By development I mean a heightening of self-awareness, an increase of autonomy, and a broadening of perspective on the world. My concern is that faculty better understand themselves and their social and organizational situation, and my hope is that such knowledge will make them better teachers, better researchers, better educators generally" (p. ix). Within this same early volume on faculty development Norbert Ralph (1973) wrote, "Development means dealing with experience in increasingly sophisticated and complex ways and being able to integrate this complexity into stable structures" (p. 62). These words still speak to us today as we face growing complexities arising from technological developments impacting our professional activities.

The second question readers might ask is what we mean by *technology*, which can mean many different things. Again, we opt for a simple understanding. Whether we use the singular form or the plural form of the word, whether or not we add an adjectival qualifier, we are referring to the hardware, software, and actualized capabilities of the computer and audio/video communication technologies as we know them in the late 1990s—e-mail; listservs; intranet; Internet; World Wide Web; CD-ROMs; audio, computer, and video conferencing; multimedia—and probably some more terms of which we have not yet even thought.

There is much discussion among us about the reform of education, the technology revolution, the Information Age, the changing paradigm. Indeed, sometimes one almost tires of hearing these and other such terms and phrases. Nonetheless, they are all important; and we would like to place another less frequently heard one into the conversations, that is, *the changing epistemology* of what we do—the examination of the ways in which we know and all the quintessential questions debated for centuries about human knowledge. Such diverse areas as feminist theory and pedagogy, our changing methods of inquiry, constructivism and postmodernism, developments in brain research and educational and cognitive psychology, the concept of reflective practice, and even quantum physics are deepening our understanding of epistemology. The new technologies provide us with the opportunity to actualize this enriched epistemological questioning and understanding. As Batson and Bass (1996) wrote, "The information technologies are changing 'where' and 'how' we think about the way we think. We will seek out those tendencies and capabilities of information technologies that connect to the current epistemology in our fields. More and more, this is epistemology not abstracted on the printed page, but experienced through the flying merge [metaphor of information highway and traffic merges]. This is epistemology in motion in the digital theater where ideas increasingly are born, socialized, matured, and remolded" (p. 45).

As we consider the changes occurring in the work and lives of faculty members and think about the related epistemological shift amidst which we find ourselves, it is a natural next step to think about the use of the technologies for the purposes of faculty development. Just as we are modifying and expanding our approaches to traditional teaching and learning, so, too, should we be considering changing the traditional approaches for the delivery of faculty development programs and services.

In 1995 Steve Gilbert, one of the leaders of our collective discussions relating to technology, posed a series of questions, one of which was for the faculty developer: "Can I help faculty adopt new approaches to teaching and new technologies at the same time?" (p. 47). Whether faculty, administrators, or faculty developers, we need to answer this question; and one would hope that faculty developers, in particular, would choose to do so with a resounding "Of course!"

One way of doing so is to use the technologies for the purposes of faculty development, which becomes learning by doing—a simple and time-honored principle. In fact, if we do not do this, we are not matching the paradigmatic and epistemological shifts to the extent both appropriate and needed. Faculty development, too, must continue to evolve. As Gaff and Justice (1978) wrote two decades ago about the role of faculty development, "[It] will change as colleges and universities adapt to changing conditions. It will be called upon to assist the overall development of institutions as they confront the challenges of excellence, equity, and efficiency. The long-term success of faculty development will depend on how well it assists both faculty members and institutions of higher learning to meet these challenges" (p. 97).

With the onslaught presented by the technology in education today, we have perhaps never before been so aware of faculty members as learners. Indeed, we are and always have been learners. That notion becomes strikingly clear, however, as we think for example of our scramble in recent years to understand something meaningful, to *learn,* about the technologies—on top of everything else we have to continue doing to meet our professional responsibilities. Thus, we can look at ourselves in a perhaps slightly new way—as adult learners. Faculty development then becomes an adult learning undertaking.

There is not agreement among the theorists, researchers, and practitioners of adult learning as to definition of adult learning, andragogy, or principles of adult learning. (See, for example, Brookfield, 1986; Knowles, 1990; Rogers, 1986.) In fact, Brookfield (1986) wrote, "There can be few intellectual quests that, for educators and trainers of adults, assume so much significance and yet contain so little promise of successful completion as the search for a general theory of adult learning" (p. 25). Nonetheless, the legitimacy of common sense enables us to identify some characteristics of adult learners and principles of adult learning that provide helpful perspectives in thinking about the impact that is the focus of these discussions on technology, faculty development, life, and work. Brookfield delineates six principles: voluntary participation, mutual respect, collaborative spirit, praxis, critical reflection, and self-direction (pp. 9–20). Knowles (1990), an earlier theorist and practitioner of adult learning, discussed such additional principles as the need to know, readiness to learn, the importance of motivation, and the role of experience (pp. 55–63). We can easily extrapolate from these principles some basic thoughts which are also informing pedagogical changes within the context of regular classroom instruction, such as cooperative/collaborative learning; undergraduate research; constructivist teaching and learning; and independent, nonlinear learning.

Application of these thoughts from the field of adult learning to faculty development within the technological context of today leads us to what we might conceptualize as "just-in-time" and on-demand delivery of faculty development programs and services, virtual faculty development, the genesis of electronic community, and self-paced faculty development. One would hope that institutionalized faculty development efforts have always been guided by the conception of the faculty member as adult learner. Recent technological developments, however, offer us new ways of extending faculty development in potentially even more effective ways and perhaps with wider impact than before the onset of the technological revolution, which is changing the way we live and work.

Guided then by several articulated assumptions and within the context of a changing epistemology and adult learning, we focus on several particularly pertinent topics. The chapter authors of this volume and I, the editor, represent diverse kinds of institutions; collectively we have a great variety of background and experience. Roger Baldwin discusses the impact of technology on faculty life and work, and its challenge to the conventional nature and structure of faculty careers. He offers ideas on the implications that the incorporation of technology has for us as individuals and for institutions. Taking this challenge further, and based on the ultimate goal of enhancing learners' experiences, Anita Gandolfo considers our traditional structures and pedagogies, the potential of technology to transform higher education, and the critical need to incorporate research on teaching and learning into decisions and applications related to technology. Instructional design is at the basis of all that we do in planning, delivering, and assessing instruction. Each of us has something on which we base our design of instruction, no matter what the instructional setting may be, even though we might not have articulated that basis for ourselves.

Frank Gillespie examines the classic model of instructional design in light of what we can now do with technology and suggests that new approaches to design are needed. Tony Di Petta brings us an international perspective from Canada and presents thoughts on the concept of electronic community—something most of us could not have even conceptualized just a few years ago. An in-depth case study of the use of technology in a rather unusual cooperative program is provided by Karen Carey and Shelly Dorn. This case study indirectly takes us to thinking about "seamless" education, working together with K–12 educators. Finally, we describe several interesting and innovative specific examples of the use of technology for the purpose of faculty development.

These thoughts are offered with the hope that the reader is invited to reflection, to affirmation of thoughts perhaps still forming, and finally to action in the effort we are all making to incorporate exciting new technological capabilities into our changing world of higher education.

Kay Herr Gillespie
Editor

References

Batson, T., and Bass, R. "Teaching and Learning in the Computer Age: Primacy of Process." *Change, 28* (2), 1996, 42–47.

Brookfield, S. D. *Understanding and Facilitating Adult Learning.* San Francisco: Jossey-Bass, 1986.

Freedman, M. (ed.). *Facilitating Faculty Development.* New Directions for Higher Education, no.1. San Francisco: Jossey-Bass, 1973.

Gaff, J. S., and Justice, D. O. "Faculty Development Yesterday, Today, and Tomorrow." *Institutional Renewal Through the Improvement of Teaching.* New Directions for Higher Education, no. 24. San Francisco: Jossey-Bass, 1978.

Gilbert, S. W. "Teaching, Learning, and Technology." *Change,* 1995, *27* (2), 46–52.

Knowles, M. *The Adult Learner: A Neglected Species.* (4th ed.) Houston: Gulf, 1990.

Ralph, N. "Stages of Faculty Development." In M. Freedman (ed.), *Facilitating Faculty Development.* New Directions for Higher Education, no.1. San Francisco: Jossey-Bass, 1973.

Rogers, A. *Teaching Adults.* Philadelphia: Open University Press, 1986.

KAY HERR GILLESPIE is editor and faculty consultant in the Office of Instructional Support and Development at the University of Georgia in Athens, Georgia. She is also professor emerita at Colorado State University.

Technology is gradually transforming higher education. In the process,
the work and careers of professors may change dramatically.

Technology's Impact on Faculty Life and Work

Roger G. Baldwin

As an early member of the baby boom generation, I am rather old to be in an awkward transitional stage. Having departed adolescence more than thirty years ago, I naively believed I could sail along until impending retirement renewed questions about my identity and sense of competence. Unfortunately, however, the pace of change in the late twentieth century does not permit such tranquility, perhaps largely due to the influence of technology. Thus, I find that I am once again in an uncomfortable stage—too old to be completely at ease with technology, yet too young to ignore it. The fact is, technology is gradually transforming higher education and the work of the academic profession. I and nearly one million colleagues (Kirshstein, Matheson, and Jing, 1997) teaching in colleges and universities must try to understand changes that are revolutionizing our daily lives and raising fundamental questions about our primary functions. This chapter explores how technology is influencing the work lives and careers of faculty in higher education through an examination of the increasingly intimate relationship between technology and the academic profession.

When I became a professor only fourteen years ago, I prepared class notes on a yellow legal pad and revised them with an eraser. When time permitted, I actually typed them on a state-of-the-art IBM Selectric. I communicated with colleagues elsewhere via telephone and mail. When I needed information for a class or research, I walked across campus to the library and thumbed through the card catalog. Today this account of my early career sounds more like an excerpt from a Victorian era Dickens novel than a description of academic life as recently as the mid-1980s.

Similarly, when a computing specialist explained the concept of electronic mail to me in the late 1970s, I had no doubt that he and his "techie" friends were completely divorced from reality. I believed there was no way computer-based communication would ever substitute for established communications.

NEW DIRECTIONS FOR TEACHING AND LEARNING, no. 76, Winter 1998 © Jossey-Bass Publishers

Now I realize that I was actually the one removed from reality. Changes were swirling about me that I had failed to perceive. Almost like Rip Van Winkle awakening from a twenty-year nap, I look around today and see a host of technological developments that are transforming what it means to be a college professor. Fax machines, e-mail, computers, the World Wide Web, and multimedia classrooms are now routine aspects of faculty life—no longer interesting curiosities but standard parts of the infrastructure of the academy and essential tools for the conduct of business.

There is no dispute that new technologies have become part of our reality in higher education. At the same time, the impact of these technologies is still being sorted out. Just how has technology changed the primary roles and work lives of professors? And how might technology change the way we work as it becomes a more fully integrated component of the academy?

Technology's Selective Impact

It is important to preface this look at technology's impact on academic life by acknowledging that the impact is not uniform. Some faculty have been affected by technology more than others, just as some endorse new teaching approaches more than others. There are differences by field and type of institution. Some schools have the resources to invest heavily in technology while others with fewer resources do not have the same capacity. Likewise, some academic fields, such as the natural sciences, mathematics, and professional areas, have been working with high-tech tools, especially computers, longer than areas such as the arts and the humanities. Hence, the transformation that technology brings to higher education may have progressed further in certain academic areas than in others.

When considering the selective impact, it is helpful to apply Rogers's (1995) model on the diffusion of innovations. According to this framework, individuals and organizations adopt innovations at different rates and play different roles in the adoption process. The key roles Rogers identifies are innovators, early adopters, laggards, change agents, and opinion leaders. Based on Rogers's scheme, we have innovators and early adopters quick to accept and experiment with novel resources such as high-tech tools. We also have the majority who accept an innovation much later in the process or who may actually resist adopting new tools.

For the purposes of this chapter, a simplified version of Rogers's scheme is useful. This version emerged from an AAHE-sponsored electronic discussion of why faculty use or resist technology ("An 'Online' Experience," 1995). It is important to distinguish between early adopters and mainstream faculty who integrate technology more slowly into their work lives. William Geoghegan of IBM, a participant in AAHE's "chat," lists characteristics that distinguish these two groups. The early adopters tend to have a strong technology focus, are visionary, like to take risks and experiment, favor revolutionary change, and are largely self-sufficient with regard to technology. In contrast, mainstream faculty are problem and process (not technology) focused; they are pragmatic or conservative and favor evolutionary change. Typically, they need significant technical support and want proven applications that will enhance their work performance, not untested tools that require risk-taking and experimentation. Geoghegan estimates that 15 percent of faculty are early adopters who enjoy trying out new technologies either for the fun of it or because they believe that the new tools will "enable breakthrough improvements in teaching and learning" ("An 'Online' Experience," 1995, p. 31). The remaining faculty members must be convinced by compelling evidence that technology will support their professional lives in meaningful ways.

It is essential to remember that technology's impact is dynamic and varied, and we focus on a moving target as we seek to understand this transformation. Although it is beneficial to draw general conclusions about the growing role technology plays in academe, we must also remember that every professor has unique experiences and feelings about technology.

Impact on Teaching

There seems to be a widespread consensus in higher education that technology has the potential to revolutionize the teaching-learning process. The evidence on how far this revolution has advanced is less clear, however. According to a University of Southern California study reported just three years ago, "Less than five percent of college and university faculty use computing to aid classroom instruction or enrich student learning" (DeSieno, 1995, p. 47). Yet the 1995 *Campus Computing* survey found "dramatic recent changes in the use of information technology in instruction" (Green, 1996, p. 26). Kenneth Green, who has conducted this important survey for eight years, reports that growing numbers of faculty across all types of institutions and disciplines are employing a wide variety of technologies in college courses. Substantial one-year increases in use continue to be found for e-mail, Internet resources, CD-ROM-based materials, multimedia, and other technology-based course applications (Green, 1997). Each application assessed in 1997 was employed in 10 percent or more of college classes. E-mail, Internet resources, and presentation handouts were used in at least 20 percent of college classes. Although Green (1996) observed that much of the technology currently in use in college instruction is "decidedly low tech," (p. 26), he concluded there has been a steady "migration of information technology into instruction" (p.28) since the early 1980s. This evidence supports the conclusion that technology has entered the instructional mainstream, but Green (1996) believes that instructional technology "has not radically transformed classrooms or the instructional activities of most faculty" (p. 28).

At present it appears that most professors use technology to supplement traditional instruction, not to redefine the instructional process. (See also Chapters Two and Three). Some evidence suggests that conditions may soon be right to stimulate the long-anticipated technology-driven instructional revolution. Green (1996) argues that the use of information technology on campuses has reached the "critical mass," which Rogers believes necessary for the adoption of an innovation to become self-sustaining.

Many advocates of reform suggest that technology calls traditional faculty instructional roles into question. In the traditional model, instruction is professor-centered with students in a secondary, often passive, role. As a 1997 *Chronicle of Higher Education* article reported, the traditional professor is course designer, lecturer, discussion moderator, and learning evaluator. New technologies challenge these roles because some aspects can be performed more effectively or efficiently using technology. For example, state-of-the-art courses employing multimedia components can be designed by expert teams of knowledge specialists and instructional technologists and then sold to individual campuses. Similarly, the information dissemination function of lecturing can be done by authorities captured technologically, thus eliminating the repetitive aspects of course instruction and freeing professors for more creative aspects of college teaching. Fuller integration of technology into college classrooms may eventually convert the college professor from a "sage on the stage" to a "guide on the side" (Young, 1997, p. A26) just as is happening with modification of teaching approaches through the introduction of cooperative or collaborative learning, for example.

According to this new conception of the instructor's role, the professor will have more time for direct student contact and individual feedback and will essentially play a supportive role as students learn to take more responsibility for their learning and collaborate with peers. In this new environment, the professor's function will be to create conditions conducive to learning, to engage students actively in the learning process, and to monitor behaviors and adjust strategies as needed to facilitate subject mastery and personal growth. In addition to being a subject matter expert, this new type of professor will need instructional technology skills, counseling skills, and a keen knowledge of group dynamics. These skills are necessary to integrate technology into the teaching-learning process and to facilitate the individualized, active, and collaborative learning strategies that new technologies can promote. As Young (1997) observed, "At issue is the basic job description of a professor" (p. A26). Compelling evidence shows that the teaching duties of the college professor are gradually changing. Other aspects of the professor's job will evolve dramatically as well.

Impact on Research and Scholarship

In comparison to the more gradual changes occurring in teaching, technology has already substantially transformed the research and scholarship component of faculty life. According to Susan Saltrick (1996), "College faculty make up one of the most plugged-in professions in their use of technology for research—and one of the most retrograde in their use of technology for teaching" (p. 59). The reason for this distinction, she argues, is that technologies such as the Internet enhance the information sharing that is a natural part of the scholarly process. In contrast, full utilization of new technologies requires major alterations in the usual work patterns associated with teaching. Hence, instructional technologies have been slower to foster change in that area of faculty job responsibility.

The array of information technologies in recent years has increased the scholarly power of professors. E-mail, fax machines, the World Wide Web, and CD-ROMs have greatly enhanced access to information sources and also increased the speed of information retrieval. Scholars used to spend long hours plowing through archival material, analyzing research data, or going through library card catalogs. In the 1990s, the same types of information can be retrieved and analyzed in seconds; and most of us enjoy the convenience of accessing library catalogues from our offices. These advanced technologies enable professors to work more quickly, to increase their overall level of research productivity, and to address research questions that heretofore would have been inconceivable because of the complexity of the data management and analysis involved.

Technology has transformed the research and scholarship component of faculty life by easing the process of collegial communication and collaboration. When choosing collaborators, faculty are no longer restricted by geography or communication limits of the telephone and mail. High speed communication is now possible using e-mail, fax, overnight mail, and voice mail (Austin and Baldwin, 1991). Specialized electronic discussion groups now abound, which just a short time ago were not possible. Technology may actually enhance the rigor of scholarship by providing unprecedented access to expertise and permitting a wider range of prepublication review and feedback than was previously possible (Van Dusen, 1997). Technology is also providing "new venues for collaboration, including electronic journals, discussion lists and conferences, database application packages, . . . and a variety of new forms of multimedia" (Batson and Bass, 1996, p. 47). Each of the new information technologies eases the process of scholarship by increasing scholars' access to colleagues, intellectual resources, and research outlets throughout the world.

Impact on Service and Outreach

In recent years there has been growing pressure to increase higher education's service to society as the demand for specialized knowledge and highly skilled personnel has grown and as calls for accountability have increased. Lynton and Elman (1987) argued more than a decade ago that professors should be more engaged in solving real world problems. Likewise, Boyer's (1990) concepts of the scholarship of integration and application advocate a larger role for faculty in applying their special knowledge and skills to resolving concrete problems. In Plater's view (1995), "Universities and colleges not only have an obligation to apply their knowledge and expertise to the solution of problems, but they have to do so in a timely fashion with immediate and demonstrable results" (p. 32).

Technology breaks down the barriers between campus and community and greatly eases the transfer of information, expertise, and resources in both directions. The transformation in the service role of faculty is still in process, however. In applied fields like business and public health, external service comprises a significant portion of the professional duties of many faculty, as is also the case for faculty at land grant institutions. In less applied fields, the service role of faculty is greatly varied. Plater believes that "As demands for service to the community increase, the number of faculty who hold appointments directly related to service will also increase" (1995, p. 32). No doubt technology will foster this change, because it makes faculty more accessible to the larger public and helps professors translate their expertise into more readily understood forms.

Special Challenges of Technology

There is little doubt that technology is a principal force gradually transforming the work and careers of professors. Because this transformation is still under way, the eventual outcome remains in doubt. It is too soon to say what academic life will be like in 2010 or 2025 as a result of technology's impact. It is not too soon, however, to see that technology has special challenges to faculty which must be addressed if the academic profession is to remain healthy and vital.

The traditional three-part academic role has been firmly in place since the beginning of this century. Teaching, scholarship, and service remain the primary faculty functions; but each is being broadened and diversified by technology. The discussion above shows technology's potential for expanding faculty duties. Technology has likewise quickened the pace of change in faculty life. An outcome of this process may be role overload or role conflict as faculty seek to perform each of their traditional duties effectively while accommodating the rapid changes in pedagogy, research methodology, and service delivery that technology stimulates. While technology enables faculty to perform tasks and achieve goals never before possible, it can also increase stress levels by adding many new responsibilities (Simpson, 1998).

Information overload is a related problem that can emerge from faculty access to sophisticated new technologies. A faculty member's job has been and remains essentially open-ended, for one can always do more to prepare for class or enhance scholarship. Thanks to e-mail, the Web, CD-ROMs, and other technology-based tools, the vastly expanded access to resources has the potential to bury academics in information. This phenomenon confronts us with important questions about information filtering, priority setting, time management, and related processes required to impose limits on information and preserve some reasonable balance in faculty life. It also has implications for teaching students to deal with information overload and to approach it critically.

Moreover, the integration of new technologies into academic life raises significant professional development challenges. Until recently, keeping pace with new developments in one's academic field was the primary professional growth concern. As the pace of knowledge production has quickened and become more specialized, this task has grown exponentially. Concurrently, the changes in faculty work fostered by technology require "that faculty develop skills not ordinarily associated with traditional instruction" (Plater, 1995, p. 29) or other standard faculty roles. Keeping pace with developments in technology and learning applications is a relatively new responsibility for professors. Designing a course that supplements or replaces lectures with on-line interactive materials "requires more technical know-how than most professors possess" (Young, 1997, p. A26).

Thus, by-products of technology confront professors with new learning and professional challenges. For example, Plater (1995) asks if faculty members feel competent to evaluate group work, manage conflict among group members, or handle a charge of plagiarism implicating a whole group. Yet technology fosters more collaborative approaches to instruction and confronts us with such novel problems. Again balance becomes an issue for faculty. How does a professor keep pace with the academic field while at the same time struggling to stay current with or catch up on rapidly changing information technologies with instructional, scholarly, or service applications?

Barriers to Technology Use

There are many compelling reasons for incorporating technology into the work lives of college and university faculty. Therefore it is particularly ironic that so many fail to employ technology in important aspects of their jobs. Articles addressing this enigma ("An 'Online' Experience," 1995; Gilbert, 1996) list numerous reasons for the failure to utilize technology fully. Among these are insufficient or obsolete hardware and software, inadequate facilities and support services, lack of time and money, an appropriate reward system, lack of information about good practice, and underestimation of the difficulty in adopting new technologies. Each factor probably contributes to the underutilization of technology and should be addressed by any institution where these conditions exist.

The overarching causes of underutilization are pinpointed by insightful observers of the educational technology scene. In Robert DeSieno's (1995) view, many faculty do not incorporate technology into key aspects of their work because for them "digital technology requires too much time and effort, supplies too many distractions, and yields too little value for the investment" (p. 47). Geoghegan sees nonadoption as primarily a matter of social and psychological factors that impede deployment of technology and believes it is not an aversion to technology itself that inhibits adoption. Rather it is "an aversion to risk, a low tolerance for discontinuous change, inadequate 'vertical' support (within the same or similar fields), and perhaps the lack of an absolutely compelling reason to buy into a new and relatively disruptive way to go about one's work" ("An 'Online' Experience," 1995, p. 31). Unlike early adopters, mainstream faculty may need to be convinced of the benefits that come from using technology. Information on success stories with technology and role models to emulate may be an essential part of this conversion process. Likewise, mainstream faculty need technical and professional support (for example, from colleagues, deans, department heads, instructional designers, computer specialists) to overcome their resistance to risk-taking with technology.

Jane Marcus ("An 'Online' Experience," 1995) offers a simple, useful formula for thinking about the conditions that will promote faculty adoption of technology:

$$A = f(R, PV, C)$$

Adoption (of technology-based innovation) is a function of available resources, perceived value the individual places on the innovation, and communication with other adopters (p. 43). This formula can serve as a diagnostic tool, which institutions, departments, or other academic units can use to assess how well their infrastructure (institutional culture, policies, resources, services, organizational structure) fosters or impedes technology experimentation and integration.

Implications of the Growing Use of Technology

This review of technology's achieved and potential impact on faculty work and the barriers to technology use has implications for current practice and future planning in higher education. It is especially important to consider these implications for faculty careers, faculty personnel policies, and faculty professional development support. The special needs of some distinctive types of faculty also deserve consideration.

Implications for Faculty Careers. The integration of new technologies into the academic workplace has greatly increased the elasticity of the academic career. Traditionally, the short academic career ladder has limited advancement options to two steps above career entry as an assistant professor. Until now, the principal alternative for professional growth within the academy has been a move to the administrative ranks as a department chair, program director, or dean. This step, however, often curtailed a professor's scholarly achievements by removal from day-to-day involvement in the disciplinary field.

One of the most attractive features of recent advances in technology is their potential to enlarge academic life by diversifying the work of faculty and expanding professional growth opportunities. Within the standard framework of teaching, research, and service, technology opens avenues for growth that can forestall unproductive career plateaus or rejuvenate faculty with a fresh challenge. Information technologies provide an array of opportunities for enhancing the teaching aspect of faculty life. No longer must professors be limited to the traditional lecture and instructional techniques that depend on a teacher and students coming together in space and time on a regular basis. In other words, technology frees professors and students to engage in teaching and learning in a much wider arena—cyberspace as well as classroom space. The professional challenges that emerge from this liberation can be daunting but also invigorating to professors seeking exciting and heretofore unprecedented growth opportunities.

Similarly, technology offers new opportunities for developing valued expertise that complements one's disciplinary specialization. Effective application of instructional technologies in specific fields will depend on the availability of skilled specialists. Faculty members who assume the role of technology specialist, instructional design specialist, or distance learning specialist in their department or college can facilitate the adoption of technology while they themselves also benefit from new professional challenges. This kind of opportunity could be especially appealing to midcareer, established professors eager to take on demanding new roles. We now have an essentially win-win situation for higher education. Increasingly sophisticated technologies require the aid of experts who can ease the application of new technology tools in specialized settings. At the same time, by assuming an important and stimulating assignment, faculty serving as specialists in technology applications add invigorating new roles to their professional lives.

Technology, likewise, loosens the limitations on an academic career imposed by geography or institutional boundaries. Throughout history, professors could teach and perform most other academic duties only where they could be physically present. Now satellite broadcast technology coupled with other information technologies enable us to teach, conduct research, and perform service in a wide variety of settings. The long reach of technology expands the venue for an academic career. Similarly, technology provides access to more diverse types of students and a broader range of research and service opportunities. It also makes resource sharing more manageable and cost effective. With high speed communications it is now feasible for professors to hold joint appointments at two or more institutions, participate in faculty exchanges, or alternate between a faculty appointment and work in a nonacademic setting such as a government agency, for-profit corporation, or private think tank. Ready access to colleagues and professional growth opportunities beyond the boundaries of one's campus also have the potential for lessening the stagnation often associated with job immobility. Technology has essentially enlarged the definition of an academic career. No longer is a professor limited to work in one institution with the same colleagues and types of students for an entire career. With imagination, careful planning, and technological support, an academic career can cover the entire planet.

Implications for Faculty Personnel Policies. Green (1996) writes of the importance of infrastructure as a critical catalyst "for innovation and for the integration of technology in instruction" (p. 26). Often institutions carefully build the technological hardware and software components of this infrastructure but give little thought to the policy component. DeSieno (1995) reports that personnel committees, curriculum committees, and college administrators have responded minimally to questions about the policy issues that technology raises.

When it is unclear how involvement with technology is valued or assessed, faculty, especially untenured faculty and faculty seeking promotion, are reluctant to experiment with technology applications.

Institutions wishing to promote faculty use of technology need policies that enhance the perceived value of incorporating technology into teaching, scholarship, and service. Certainly tenure and promotion policies should address technology questions, especially what types of technology-based activities and products (for example, software, on-line publications, course units) may be submitted for review and how they will be evaluated.

Leave policies should also be reexamined in light of technology advances. Traditionally, academic leaves and sabbaticals have been restricted to specialized research projects or learning in one's area of specialization. In the new academic climate fostered by technology, institutions should consider whether faculty may instead devote a leave to studying technology in general or applications of technology in a professor's disciplinary field.

Ultimately, technology raises questions about the primary functions of a professor. Should all professors be expected to engage in teaching, research, and service continuously throughout their careers, or is some form of differentiated staffing now more appropriate? A differentiated staffing policy will enable professors to concentrate their efforts in areas of principal interest and strength or areas where they wish to develop new expertise. For example, a professor could reduce her regular teaching load and serve some time primarily as an instructional technology specialist or instructional design consultant. This type of policy would also build more flexibility into the academic career. Above all, such a staffing policy would acknowledge, as Boyer (1990) suggested, that it is no longer appropriate to expect all faculty to perform exactly the same functions throughout academic life. A differentiated staffing policy would recognize the reality of the different roles faculty play in higher education in the late twentieth century rather than pretend they do not exist.

Implications for Faculty Professional Development Support. Capitalizing on higher education's major investment in technology requires carefully planned professional development support for faculty. As stated previously, full utilization of new technologies requires professors to develop new skills and assume new functions. Early adopters among the faculty may forge ahead independently into the mysterious world of technology. In contrast, mainstream faculty must have a support system that will ease their movement into unfamiliar territory. Hence, institutions should keep their mainstream faculty in mind as they devise professional development policies and programs.

Assuming the technological infrastructure (hardware and software) is in place in an institution, attention to the social and psychological aspects of adopting technology should be a high priority. It is critical that mainstream faculty have access to training, time to learn and work with the technology, and adequate support (technological, pedagogical, and scholarly) when it is needed. Examples of innovative and realistic applications of technology as well as the use of technology for the delivery of faculty development programs, services, and activities may help to convince and enable mainstream faculty to join the ranks of technology users. Demonstrations of successful applications may be more useful than dozens of articles or speeches testifying to the benefits of technology. Marcus's equation on the adoption of innovations suggests that communication with technology users is an important variable in encouraging faculty adoption of technology ("An 'Online' Experience," p. 43). To provide this support, institutions will need to "challenge existing patterns of work and specialization on campuses" (DeSieno, 1995, p. 48). Deans, department chairs, and faculty developers must foster more faculty collaboration, encouraging faculty who use technology in their teaching or scholarship to work closely with those "who are just beginning and to share their pedagogical [and other professional] experiences" (DeSieno, 1995, p. 3) with less technologically competent colleagues. In some cases this would be a reverse form of mentoring where younger, more technologically sophisticated junior faculty assist their senior colleagues. Adequate support for the full integration of technology will require academic units or whole institutions to think and work more like close-knit, integrated communities (DeSieno, 1995). Fundamentally, as technology advances further into academe, it may challenge the "lone wolf" or "independent entrepreneur" professorial model. To succeed in a technologically advanced era, professors may need to become more interdependent and mutually supportive.

Not surprisingly, technology can provide some of the professional development support needed to facilitate wider use of technology. The Internet and the World Wide Web are now playing a major role in the delivery of professional development. For example, listservs, newsgroups, and e-mail discussion groups provide asynchronous forums for electronic communication and professional support (Van Dusen, 1997). If assistance from colleagues is not readily available on campus, a professor can quickly find help in cyberspace. Initially, professors may need aid, however, to identify such resources. Workshops, demonstrations, or tutorial sessions can introduce academics to the wide range of professional development resources accessible through the computer.

Faculty Who Present Special Challenges. As institutions seek to promote the application of new technologies, two particular faculty groups present special professional development challenges. The distinctive circumstances and needs of contingent faculty (part-time and full-time faculty off the tenure track) and faculty who resist adopting technology deserve attention. Contingent faculty represent an increasingly large segment of the professoriate. Approximately 42 percent of all instructional faculty and staff are in part-time positions. Among faculty in full-time positions, about 24 percent are not eligible for tenure (Kirshstein, Matheson, and Jing, 1997). Chester Finn (1998) believes that the numbers of contingent faculty will continue to grow as institutions try to enhance flexibility in response to shifting market forces. Technology-resistant faculty are a concern for a related reason. In a rapidly changing environment these faculty have the potential to be devalued and marginalized.

Contingent faculty often are not full-fledged members of an academic community (Gappa and Leslie, 1993). By definition, their relationship to their institution is not permanent. In many cases, they receive lower salaries than tenure-eligible counterparts and have access to fewer professional amenities, including technology resources. Support for professional development in the form of travel funds, sabbatical leaves, and assistance with technological applications often is not codified for contingent faculty and may be available only on an ad hoc basis when provided by a sympathetic department chair or dean. Given the rapid changes in academic life that technology is fostering, this lack of support can exaggerate status differences between faculty who are eligible for tenure and those who are not. Likewise, limited access to technology support raises quality concerns for a substantial segment of the academic profession and the students they teach. The implication is clear and simple. Higher education institutions must ensure that contingent faculty, along with their permanent colleagues, receive appropriate professional development support so that they, too, may keep pace with new technological applications.

Faculty who are slow to integrate technology into their work present a different sort of challenge. They may need carefully crafted support to overcome their reluctance to adopt useful technologies. For example, Geoghegan and Havice observed that "having early adopters serve as role models can backfire if novices are put off by their own sense of inadequacy" ("An 'Online' Experience," 1995, p. 44). In some cases, efforts to build technology competence and use may have to be designed carefully to meet the distinctive needs of individual faculty.

Resistant faculty pose an important question: Should all faculty be encouraged to incorporate technology into their work? This question could provoke a heated debate on most campuses today, and that debate has already begun at some institutions. Van Dusen (1997) cautions against pitting the technology enthusiasts against the traditionalists. He recognizes that pressure is growing on traditionalists to adopt technology. Yet Van Dusen concludes from his analysis of the "virtual campus" that at least for teaching, "for the foreseeable future a wide range of classroom activities from the traditional lecture to virtual reality experiments will continue to serve the needs of students" (p. 122). He believes that room remains in higher education for both "techies" and "laggards."

Indeed, some analysts believe that technology skeptics perform a useful function on their campuses (Bromley, 1998; Neal, 1998). Often institutions acquire a new or updated technology because it exists or because the competition already has it. The result is that technology frequently drives the curriculum rather than vice versa (Bromley, 1998). "Most attempts to criticize the roles of technology are answered with ad hominem charges of 'Luddite.'" (Crawford, cited in Bromley, 1998, p. 22). In our unbounded enthusiasm, it is easy to forget that the impact of technology on the academy as a whole and faculty in particular remains unclear. Many questions should be asked as higher education progresses further in its romance with technology. For example, "what educational priorities will be compromised to pay the escalating cost of acquiring new computer technology. . .?" (Bowers, 1998, p.51). Reluctant faculty confront their colleagues and academic leaders with the need to consider such important questions. Just as technology's innovators and early adopters can show us how to integrate technology, technology's laggards and Luddites can help us consider why and when we can best employ technology to enhance academic work and educational quality. Likewise, skeptics force us to consider when it is best not to replace an effective practice or a human touch with a shiny new technological tool (Van Dusen, 1998).

Conclusion

As a member of the baby boom generation, I am accustomed to traveling through major life stages with large groups of my contemporaries. As a mid-career professor in the midst of a major transition stimulated by technology, I also have a lot of company. The vast mainstream of the American professoriate can be found somewhere in this stage of transition.

There is little doubt that new technologies are facilitating a reexamination and redefinition of academic life. Some of that change has already taken place. Much more is likely to happen in the next ten to twenty years. A quick perusal of titles in the *Chronicle of Higher Education*'s Information Technology section confirms that we are a long way from resolving all of the questions and dilemmas technology poses. "Historians Form New Organization on Technology in Teaching and Research" (Guernsey, 1998, p. A30), "Those Who Publish on Line Fear They Suffer in Tenure Reviews" (Guernsey, 1997, p. A21), and "Skeptical Academics See Perils in Information Technology" (Young, 1998, p. A29) are just a few examples. Each heading speaks to the possibilities as well as the anxieties emerging as technology moves further into our professorial work and daily lives.

From our vantage point in the late 1990s, we cannot be certain where technology will take the academic profession. Based on experience to date, however, we can be certain that technology enlarges academic life and makes it more flexible and dynamic. It is important to monitor future technological developments with the rigor of a skeptic. Higher education and the academic profession should adopt only those technological advances that enable us to enhance educational quality and better serve society. At the same time, professors and the organizations that represent them (for example, the American Association of University Professors, disciplinary societies) should resist defensiveness and remain open to positive changes that new information technologies make possible.

With careful planning and supportive institutions, technology will enable professors to build more exciting and far-reaching careers than were possible at any previous time in the long history of the professoriate. Our society has a greater need for knowledge and advanced skills than ever before. Technology, carefully applied, has the ability to move educators and scholars to the very center of society. From this position academics can participate fully in shaping the new century. Faculty should, however, advance cautiously into the new world that technology makes possible, being careful not to fall for every technological trinket or fad that becomes available. But they should advance with a sense of optimism. If academics assume a leadership role in applying technology within institutions of higher learning, these exciting new tools will permit us to build a very bright future for ourselves and our students as well as for our entire system of higher education.

References

Austin, A. E., and Baldwin, R. G. *Faculty Collaboration: Enhancing the Quality of Scholarship and Teaching.* ASHE-ERIC Higher Education Report no. 7. Washington, D.C.: Graduate School of Education and Human Development, George Washington University, 1991.

Batson, T., and Bass, R. "Teaching and Learning in the Computer Age: Primacy of Process." *Change,* 1996, *28* (2), 42–47.

Bowers, C. A. "The Paradox of Technology: What's Gained and Lost?" *Thought and Action,* 1998, *14* (1), 49–57.

Boyer, E. *Scholarship Reconsidered: Priorities of the Professoriate.* Princeton, N.J.: Carnegie Foundation for the Advancement of Teaching, 1990.

Bromley, H. "How to Tell If You Really Need the Latest Technology." *Thought and Action,* 1998, *14* (1), 21–28.

DeSieno, R. "Netlaw: The Faculty and Digital Technology." *Educom Review,* 1995, *30* (4), 46–48.

Finn, C. E. "Today's Academic Market Requires a New Taxonomy of Colleges." *Chronicle of Higher Education,* Jan. 9, 1998, p. B4.

Gappa, J. M., and Leslie, D. W. *The Invisible Faculty: Improving the Status of Part-Timers in Higher Education.* San Francisco: Jossey-Bass, 1993.

Gilbert, S. W. "Making the Most of a Slow Revolution." *Change,* 1996, *28* (2), 10–23.

Green, K. C. "The Coming Ubiquity of Information Technology." *Change,* 1996, *28* (2), 24–28.

Green, K. C. "The 1997 National Survey of Information Technology in Higher Education." [http://ericir.syr.edu/Projects/Campus_computing/1997/index.html]. 1997.

Guernsey, L. "Those Who Publish On Line Fear They Suffer in Tenure Reviews." *Chronicle of Higher Education,* June 6, 1997, p. A21.

Guernsey, L. "Historians Form New Organization on Technology in Teaching and Research." *Chronicle of Higher Education,* May 8, 1998, p. A30.

Kirshstein, R., Matheson, N., and Jing, Z. *Instructional Faculty and Staff in Higher Education Institutions: Fall 1987 and Fall 1992,* NCES 97–447. 1993 National Study of Postsecondary Faculty, NSOPF–93. Washington, D.C.: National Center for Education Statistics, U.S. Department of Education, 1997.

Lynton, E., and Elman, S. *New Priorities for the University: Meeting Society's Needs for Applied Knowledge and Competent Individuals.* San Francisco: Jossey-Bass, 1987.

Neal, E. "Using Technology in Teaching: We Need to Exercise Healthy Skepticism." *Chronicle of Higher Education,* June 19, 1998, pp. B4–B5.

"An 'Online' Experience." *Change,* 1995, *27* (2), 28–45.

Plater, W. M. "Future Work: Faculty Time in the 21st Century." *Change,* 1995, *27* (3), 22–33.

Rogers, E. *Diffusion of Innovations.* (4th ed.) New York: Free Press, 1995.

Saltrick, S. "A Campus of Our Own: Thoughts of a Reluctant Conservative." *Change,* 1996, *28* (2), 58–62.

Simpson, R. "The Overwhelming Nature of Higher Education." *Innovative Higher Education,* 1998, *22* (4), 267–269.

Van Dusen, G. C. *The Virtual Campus: Technology and Reform in Higher Education.* ASHE-ERIC Higher Education Report no. 1. Washington, D.C.: School of Education and Human Development, George Washington University, 1997.

Van Dusen, G. C. "Technology: Higher Education's Magic Bullet." *Thought and Action,* 1998, *14* (1), 59–67.

Young, J. R. "Rethinking the Role of the Professor in an Age of High-Tech Tools." *Chronicle of Higher Education,* Oct. 3, 1997, p. A26.

Young, J. R. "Skeptical Academics See Perils in Information Technology." *Chronicle of Higher Education,* May 8, 1998, p. A29.

ROGER G. BALDWIN is professor of higher education at the College of William and Mary in Williamsburg, Virginia.

The focus of higher education institutions is on the application of technology to students—undergraduate and graduate—and the traditional structures and pedagogies employed in the education of those students. We are already changing, so we might as well do it consciously.

Brave New World? The Challenge of Technology to Time-Honored Pedagogies and Traditional Structures

Anita Gandolfo

A few weeks ago, I noticed construction at a cluster of vacant stores in my neighborhood with a sign proclaiming the opening of a movie theater. Later I learned from a newspaper article that this local cinema is part of a trend; movie theaters are sprouting up throughout the counties north of Manhattan, as "going to the movies" seems to have been rediscovered (Berger, 1998). Being of a certain age, I recall how the advent of television sounded the death knell to the movie theater in the early 1950s and the later prediction that the VCR would seal the coffin. Yet here in 1998, with Blockbuster Video on almost every corner, the neighborhood movie theater remains alive and well.

Thus, while enthusiasts announce the "brave new world" of higher education through technology, predicting the demise of the campus as we know it, my own traditional education provides a caveat. In Shakespeare's *The Tempest,* the isolated and innocent Miranda, seeing a group of men for the first time, exclaims, "How beauteous mankind is! O brave new world / That has such people in't!" Her more experienced, cynical father Prospero responds, "'Tis new to thee." To an experienced educator, the chorus proclaiming the "brave new world" of technology that will transform higher education reflects a Miranda-like naïveté.

Note: The views expressed in this chapter represent those of the author and in no way represent the official position of the U.S. Military Academy, U.S. Army, or Department of Defense.

The Challenge to Tradition

Unfortunately, differing viewpoints on the use of technology for instruction in higher education reflect less the quaint charm of Shakespeare's father and daughter than antagonists in an increasingly vituperative war. Most of the combatants defending the value of technology to effect a learning revolution employ the rhetoric of business, proclaiming savings and efficiencies to compensate for declining budgets. When Carol Twigg, vice president of Educom, writes about the need to "realize productivity gains in higher education" through "fundamental changes in management, organization and human resources" (1995, p. 51), it is clear that her language would alienate many professors. They, in turn, employ rhetoric that is inimical to the "bottom line" thinking of management specialists. For example, when the educator Samuel Williamson points out that "education and learning at their best are not training, not just learning, but the total experience of maturation, reflection, and of intellectual, even spiritual development" (1996, p. 4), he is not simply arguing a different position, but articulating a different paradigm from that underlying Carol Twigg's comment.

A recent article in *The Chronicle of Higher Education* illustrates these differing paradigms in recounting the conflict between professors at the University of Washington and its governor's commission on the future of higher education. While commission members speak of the "brave new world of digital education," faculty members refer to "quixotic ideas" that they fear may harden into "disastrous policies" and urge the governor to "support learning as a human and social practice, an enrichment of soul and mind, the entitlement of all citizens in a democracy, and not a profit-making commodity to be offered on the cheapest terms to the highest bidder" (Monaghan, 1998, p. A23).

In a time of crisis for higher education as issues of spiraling costs, access, and accountability generate concern, technology presents both danger and opportunity. Undoubtedly, there is opportunity; the effective use of technology has the potential to improve and enhance learning. Just as assuredly there is the danger that the wrongheaded adoption of various technologies apart from a sound grounding in educational research and practice will result, and indeed in some instances has already resulted, in costly additions to an already expensive enterprise without any value added. That is, technology applications must be consonant with what is known about the nature of learning and must be assessed to ensure that they are indeed enhancing learners' experiences.

That this is not happening in the currently polarized environment is eminently clear. In a recent essay, Ed Neal, Director of the Center for Teaching and Learning at the University of North Carolina at Chapel Hill, commented on the pressures placed on faculty members, citing "such absurdities as administrators' requiring all faculty members to post their syllabi on the World Wide Web or requiring all students to demonstrate competency in computer use, whether or not it is relevant in their fields" (1998, p. B4). Interestingly, the *New York Times* recently featured an essay by a computer professional who pointed out that she and many other pioneers in programming and software engineering in the 1970s were liberal arts graduates who were self-taught in programming. It was her traditional education, she asserted, that provided the resources for learning the new language of programming. "We had all taught ourselves computing. For us, it was just one more difficult subject to learn. No one was intimidated by learning another computer language—or anything else for that matter. What we knew was how to learn, which is all that one can hang on to in a profession in which change is relentless" (Ullman, 1998, A21).

Nevertheless, at a time when college graduates are failing basic literacy tests, academia is focusing ever more attention on computer literacy. The 1997 National Survey of Information Technology in Higher Education reports "growing numbers of campuses imposing IT requirements on their students" (Green, 1997, p. 2). Many educators would argue that if our young people are to flourish in a technological world, it is not only keyboarding skills they need; rather, they must be "resourceful, adaptable, questioning, and open-minded," and that it is "mainly through the study of history, philosophy, literature, science, and the arts that people's minds are opened to change and to new possibilities" (Postman, 1995, p. 10).

The polarized views expressed over the place of technology reflect differing views on the nature and purpose of education. Nancy S. Dye, President of Oberlin College, recently pointed out that "virtual higher education is the kind of quick technology fix Americans have always found deeply appealing" (1998, p. 11). She then explains her view of human interaction as central to the educational process: "We're very much in the business of educating citizens. We're very much in the business of furthering knowledge, and we know that the best teaching and learning happens in relationships, face to face" (p. 11). What we're seeing is often not a "paradigm shift" but a clash of competing paradigms.

If this controversy between the Prosperos and Mirandas of the digital university is to be resolved, it will be only insofar as it inspires educators to examine what we claim to be doing and how it can be done best. That is, the use of technology for instruction should provide an occasion for educators to ask how these tools can help us with our basic task of instruction and redefinition of that task. As a life-long teacher currently engaged in faculty development, my primary interest is the practical aspects of improving learning. Thus, although instructional technology is a vast topic, generating theoretical ideas about the future shape of the educational enterprise, the scope of this chapter is the challenge of the current moment in higher education. Undeniably, technology has the potential to transform teaching and learning; but just as undeniably, our faculty and traditions have demonstrated the ability to persist in the face of other challenges.

Traditional Structures and Pedagogies

Our concern, then, is about the application of technology to the students—undergraduate and graduate—and the traditional structures and pedagogies employed in the education of those students. These students may be typical eighteen-to twenty-two-year-olds or nontraditional working adults. Their academic lives are organized according to semesters, trimesters, or quarters; and they take courses organized by credit hours, with a certain number of credit hours stipulated as prerequisite for the degree. Faculty professional lives are similarly organized by the academic calendar and course assignments. And despite the interest in forms of active learning and service learning, lecture and discussion persist as the standard classroom experience of most undergraduates.

For the faculty developer, whose "students" are the faculty members, there are similar traditional structures and pedagogies. Time is divided according to the academic calendar with activities subordinated to one's classroom responsibilities, and events are timed to avoid conflict with instructors' obligations to students. Most faculty development centers offer workshops and seminars, seeking to engender conversations about teaching and learning through these events. Faculty students also often experience lecture or discussion as the instructional mode for these faculty development events. And just as most faculty members spend some time advising or tutoring students individually, most faculty developers offer confidential consultations to their faculty students.

Enter Technology

Into this traditional world of academia, technology has arrived less as the invited guest than the unwelcome stranger. Acquired by necessity to provide students with the tools needed in a technological society, hardware, software, and their maintenance have become an increasing financial burden to academe. It is hardly surprising, then, that in many instances administrative pressure to use technology has coalesced into opposition by faculty groups (Noble, 1998, p. 10).

Yet while wars are being waged over technology, its use in the classroom seems to be rising steadily. The 1997 National Survey of Information Technology in Higher Education reports an increase in college courses that make use of e-mail (32.8 percent in 1997, up from 8 percent in 1994). The survey also indicates that only 13.4 percent of all college courses use some form of multimedia resources, but that number is up from 4 percent in 1994 (Green, 1997, p. 1). This is in spite of the fact that the report adds that the "vast majority" of colleges and universities are sending "a clear if somewhat punitive message to faculty: do more with technology, but learn the skills on your own time and do it in addition to your other professional responsibilities" (Green 1997, p. 2).

On the other hand, faculty resistance may be less to using technology than what they perceive as the drift toward the world of virtual education. It often seems that what is valued in using technology for instruction is not necessarily what is valuable for student learning. One good example is the perception of the Internet as vital for all classes because of the access to information it provides. Yet there is scant mention of the need to provide the conceptual tools allowing students to function in our information-rich environment. In a 1996 presentation at the annual conference of the Middle States Association of Colleges and Schools, one librarian cited studies that document the "dismal abilities of our students, even at the most basic levels," to properly match their retrieval needs with the appropriate computer retrieval system (Oberman, 1996).

Moreover, as any faculty member who has searched the Internet for information relative to a course can attest, the Web is replete with as much bogus material as accurate information. Traditional courses in research methods need to be revamped to include the issues raised by the use of technology, and such instruction should be a prerequisite for students who are expected to use the Internet in their courses. This is a challenge faculty members should address, but the technophiles are generally silent on these issues. For example, the National Survey of IT in Higher Education reports on whether or not college courses make use of the Internet but never inquires whether (or how) students are instructed in doing research on the Internet (Green, 1997).

Technology and Teaching

While surveys show a continued rise in the numbers of courses using technology, they do not reflect the employment of the technology; and individual faculty members developing technology applications in isolation can be staggeringly myopic. A few years ago, I attended a conference on the use of technology for instruction. At one session, a humanities professor explained his use of a Web page to enhance his large lecture classes. His Web page was attractively designed, but its text seemed more suited to individual student study than class presentation. In addition, the professor admitted that few of his students had personal computers, so the value of the Web page outside of class was limited.

During the question period, I asked what seemed the logical question: "Why did you choose to use this particular technology to enhance your lectures?" His response was initially puzzling. "I had heard about the Web and decided to make a page, and when I surveyed the students after the first semester, they all liked it." When I asked my next question, it was his turn to be puzzled. "What type of visuals were you using for class before the Web page?" After looking at me quizzically for a moment, he replied, "Nothing; I just lectured."

This incident remains with me because it is not atypical of earnest faculty members attempting to use technology in their teaching. The actual use of technology may be proceeding recklessly without much reflection on the nature of learning that it purports to be addressing. I doubt that my humanities professor would have dared to give a conference presentation in his discipline that was as lacking in basic research methodology as was this presentation.

The incident also exemplifies the interface of technology with traditional structures and pedagogies. In subsequent conversation, I learned that the professor traditionally lectured to large numbers of students and that he had developed the Web site because he had heard a lot about the World Wide Web and was "interested in it." Since his school provided support for creating Web pages, he had decided to take advantage of that assistance. He himself, however, had never learned much more than how to click the mouse to get the page to appear. Moreover, he had no knowledge of other ways to create presentation graphics. This professor had apparently decided to use technology without analyzing its value for his purposes—indeed, he did not seem to think he needed any instructional goal other than to "use technology." His assessment of its effectiveness was similarly ill-conceived—"the students liked it."

Yes, he has provided something that certainly enhances the standard lecture. One point to note, however, is that the "value added" claimed for technology was, in fact, available to him long ago—with an overhead projector, for example. Often the positive uses of technology simply validate what research in teaching and learning has long indicated—in this case, that visual learners are ill-served in the traditional lecture. One does not necessarily need advanced technology to use visuals effectively. His usage of technology might have appeared innovative, yet it is ancillary to the traditional lecture standard in place since the Middle Ages. The unfortunate reality is that all this expensive equipment may do little to enhance student learning if we do not consider its capabilities in relationship to our traditional structures and pedagogies.. Like the Internet itself, the use of technology for instruction generates much discussion with all too little basis in scholarship; and it is relatively easy to focus on surface rather than substance.

Moreover, this professor may possibly reap a reward for his compliance. Having professors who "use the Web" in courses can be a selling point to students and parents. Faculty resistance to technology is hardly surprising, since there is little incentive for any of them to seriously explore the complexities of learning in order to develop a different model for instruction. A recent essay in *College Teaching* provides guidelines for "Lecturing with Technology," indicating that my humanities professor is becoming normative, as the authors herald the brave new world of "no more lectures using chalkboards and transparencies" (Nantz and Lundgren, 1998, p. 53).

"We found that more information could be covered using computer slide presentations, but there is a temptation to use too many slides. Each time a new slide was shown, the students would begin a flurry of note-taking to take down all of the information on the slide; therefore it was fruitless to say anything in the first few minutes of each new slide" (p. 55).

Three years ago Stephen Ehrmann cogently pointed out that the "broadcast" style of traditional lecturing has proven ineffectual with contemporary learners, and there will be no improvement "if we continue to teach over computer and video networks just as we have in traditional classrooms" (1995, p. 42). Yet what this article (Nantz and Lundgren, 1998) offers is advice on how to "teach over computer and video networks just as we have in traditional classrooms."

The Need for Collaboration

In a recent essay, Peter Ewell discussed technology-enhanced instruction as the latest among the "many banners" that have been raised as solutions for the improvement of higher education. In explaining the failure of various initiatives, Ewell offers significant insight: "They have been implemented without a deep understanding of what 'collegiate learning' really means and the specific circumstances and strategies that are likely to promote it" (Ewell, 1997, 3). If one thinks again of my humanities professor, this comment rings true.

If seen as a catalyst rather than a panacea, technology has potential for improving—indeed transforming—instruction. Unfortunately, the current climate often privileges the "quick fix" and easy solutions (Carr, Jonassen, Litzinger, and Marra, 1998, 14). For any new initiative to succeed in transforming higher education, Peter Ewell suggests that institutions must "engage themselves far more deeply in well-informed discussions about the characteristics and sources of higher learning" (p. 3). And Stephen Ehrmann (1995) echoes this need, adding, however, that this is unfortunately what is typically absent (p. 43). While my humanities professor had technical support, his autonomy was carefully observed. And if there is a single "tradition" that impedes the development of new ways of understanding learning, it is the radical isolation of most higher education faculty members in their much valued autonomy. The collaborative, discussion model (as in the "Teaching, Learning, Technology Roundtable" developed and promoted by Steve Gilbert for the American Association for Higher Education) is essential if technology is to be transformative rather than additive.

Change is all too frequently absent from the average faculty member's lexicon, less from recalcitrance than from naïveté. That is, the average faculty member believes that the instructional methodology is as much a part of the discipline as the subject matter. As illustration, I offer this recent conversation with a computer science colleague. One day he commented to me that he and others in his department were concerned about our dean's emphasis on active-learning strategies. He said that "traditionally" students learned computer science from reading the textbook and listening to lectures, and he felt that his discipline did not need different strategies. I asked whether he had found any difference in student learning in recent years, and he answered, "Oh, yes. We've noticed for the past five or six years that somehow the students just don't 'get it' as well." Yet, in spite of that observation, no one considered experimenting with different strategies for instruction. While I understand the danger in generalizing from the anecdotal, this conversation is illustrative of the general adherence to traditional structures that abounds throughout higher education. There is a need for educators (administrators and professors) to identify a technology vision at their institutions that is consonant with their idea of what teaching and learning is all about. Only with such a vision can short-term and long-range planning for technology be discussed with any degree of agreement.

A Vision for Technology

The situation at the United States Military Academy is instructive. In the mid-1980s when it became apparent that our cadets would serve in an increasingly technological army, each entering student acquired a desktop PC; and West Point began the development of an increasingly robust networked environment. The idea was that simply using the tools of technology in courses would create a comfort and familiarity with technology that would prepare cadets for the future. Gradually, technology was incorporated where essential to the subject matter in specific fields; and others experimented with the use of technology to improve learning. After several years, an assessment of the situation resulted in the development and publication of a vision for technology at the Academy.

Developing this vision caused us to examine the nature of learning as well as the various sites for student learning. We concluded that the classroom is principally the site for the human interaction we deem essential to education. As Dye notes, "Excellence in education happens in relationships" (1998, p. 11). However, we also observed that in some classes we spend time explaining procedures that students could learn as well or better with technology because the material cannot be easily mastered from traditional textual sources. Hence, we focus on the development of technological resources for learning guidance in the barracks—helping cadets learn the principles of map reading, for example, through an interactive program or having them do the preparation for their chemistry labs through computer simulation rather than detailed instructions in class. In addition, we've experienced the power of computer-generated graphics to assist students in understanding abstractions. Now all classrooms have computer projection capability, and the presence of this technology has inspired humanists to explore how technology can be useful in their fields. We are proceeding cautiously with the understanding that technology is a tool that we are learning to use for instruction and that the critical question is: "Why am I using it—that is, what is gained in student learning?"

Having such an institutionally specific shared vision is essential to meeting the challenge of technology. In American higher education, the faculty traditionally controls the curriculum, and any top-down initiative impacting the delivery of instruction must have faculty support. The entire life of the collegiate institution is organized to support the traditional model of instruction, so unless faculty members are engaged in working with technology to create change, there is little hope of substantial benefit.

From Vision to Reality

Technological innovations will remain localized and have little overall impact without full faculty support. The problem is that there is too little administrative impulse for this transformative value of technology, since rather than cutting costs and generating revenue, real transformation of traditional instructional practices is going to "cost long hours and big bucks" (Ehrmann, 1995, p. 42).

Change will occur if the introduction of technology is guided by an institutional vision for its use in teaching and learning that is rooted in sound instructional principles. As a faculty developer, I consider any faculty interest in using technology an opportunity to introduce critical teaching-learning questions. For example, my humanities professor might have begun by asking key questions. *Why* do I want to use technology? *What* does it have to offer to enhance students' learning? If he had decided that computer projection could provide striking visuals to complement lectures, he would then have investigated to determine *what* technology was most suited to his purposes. Since his purpose was to create something solely for the lecture, simple presentation graphics would serve his purpose.

Finally, with the goal of enhancing learning, he would naturally have sought to assess the learning outcome beyond student satisfaction. Perhaps he would try to document more depth in examination responses or papers compared to those from previous years when there were no visuals. Or he might try to determine whether students were better able to take notes in class, thus better able to study course material. Yes, the students' satisfaction is a positive indicator, but he could have asked, "If you find the use of computer graphics to augment the lecture helpful to your learning of the material, please explain how it helps."

Even in the systematic approach I've described, however, technology does not so much challenge as augment traditional structures. If technology is indeed going to have a significant positive impact, it must be used in conjunction with what is known about learning to foster improvement. This is the approach of Arthur Chickering and Stephen Ehrmann in discussing the value of technology in relation to the well-known "Seven Principles for Good Practice in Undergraduate Education"(1996). As they helpfully point out, if "learning" is considered simply the student's regurgitation of pre-packaged information, it makes little difference whether the delivery of that information is through a standard college lecture by a professor or via a computer program (p. 6). The only value of technology for instruction is if it enhances learning in ways that are not otherwise available. For example, if, as the first of the Seven Principles asserts, contact between students and faculty encourages learning, any technology that improves the frequency and quality of that contact should prove beneficial. Hence, e-mail can promote learning, perhaps even more effectively than direct contact, since the screen is a more neutral zone than the faculty member's office.

Challenge and Transformation

When students and instructor are linked, the ability of technology to transform traditional structures is immediately evident. We easily transcend the confines of the classroom and the class hour through electronic interaction with students. As with all tools for instruction, however, e-mail must be used judiciously. If an instructor relies on e-mail to compensate for poor planning and simply sends continuous messages about the course, students can "turn off" their responsiveness to those messages. On the other hand, the instructor who uses e-mail to provide learning guidance that can help students with their class preparation reaps the benefits of student preparation for class and of their appreciation for the instructor's interest in their learning.

Again, the key point is that technology must be used judiciously along with good instructional methodology. One information technology administrator I know wants to ensure that faculty members on his campus are available to students twenty-four hours a day via the Internet. He asserts that the student working on a paper at midnight and confronting a problem should be able to send a query off to the instructor and should have a reply before the first class of the day. I am unconvinced that this is a value for learning. It seems to me that the very purpose of term papers and projects is the student's independent struggle with the material and that technology that fosters student dependence on the instructor is not an advance. Hence, for each specific assignment an instructor should decide on the balance of support necessary for learning and the independence of the student. As with all technology, just because we *can* do it, doesn't mean that we *should* do it. Again, well-informed discussions among faculty colleagues will help provide the basis for intelligent use of technology for instruction.

From the faculty development perspective, the problem is in generating those "well-informed discussions." As we read over and over again in the literature, "the current school model is generations old, and its age is showing" (Bray, 1995, p. 3); but higher education faculty members, by and large, see no problem with the time-honored pedagogies. There is a lot of talk about student-centered learning, but the lecture mode is alive and well on most campuses— and now it is being enhanced by computer graphics. If technology is simply grafted onto the traditional structures of academe, we gain the appearance of advance in education without substantial advance in student learning. As Twigg (1995) also said, "we continue to operate more or less as we have done in the past, asking the same staff to do the same things in the same way" (p. 51).

My own experience suggests that by working in a technologically enhanced environment, guided by sound principles of teaching and learning, we will gradually reveal to ourselves a new paradigm. Traditional structures and pedagogies will evolve, as we "see" a new way of dong things because we've already enacted it. When I began the Center for Teaching Excellence (CTE) at the U.S. Military Academy four years ago, I instituted many traditional aspects of faculty development programs.

Gradually, because we are all networked, I began to use my computer to extend contact with faculty members. For example, each of our "brown bag" session topics is offered three times to accommodate faculty schedules, so I began summarizing the three discussions and distributing the summary via e-mail to all participants. Recently, faculty members suggested that I also post these summaries on the CTE Web page. When I do workshops, I find it fruitful to have a feedback form that includes "one question remaining that I'd like answered." I answer all those questions by e-mail to participants. Faculty responses to this practice have been positive.

In the early days, I envisioned consultations as face-to-face meetings with individual faculty members; but many faculty members at other locations find it easier to "consult" via e-mail. I also use the Web page to offer faculty members technology tools for their own classes. Our section on "Cadet Feedback" provides a mechanism for interim course feedback as well as learning assessment (see Chapter Six). Departments have created links to their own department home pages to integrate these instruments more easily into their courses. Through technology, the CTE is having a far greater impact on our faculty members than we would have in the traditional structure of a separate, centralized unit that depended principally on faculty attendance at events.

Interestingly, we may be transforming the basic paradigm in a positive way. Several years ago, Tom Angelo wrote about the ineffectiveness of many faculty development programs, citing the "additive approach to learning" that was common in higher education. In that approach, learning for students is equated with courses taken and credit hours accumulated, while "development" for faculty is measured by workshops or lectures attended. While students are usually compliant in the additive approach, needing the credits for the diploma, faculty development events are sometimes sparsely populated because of constraints of time and logistics (Angelo, 1994, p. 3). What can happen with the increased use of technology in faculty development is that faculty members begin to feel "connected" electronically, whether or not they ever attend specific faculty development events.

Technology, however, has not led to a "virtual" CTE in which I remain at my desk, delivering workshops electronically. Faculty preference is still for human interaction. In fact, our annual assessment indicates that events involving human interaction are the most requested parts of our program. It seems that the electronic activities are experienced as an extension of, but not desired as a substitute for, face-to-face interactions.

I believe that this experience may be at the heart of some faculty members' reluctance to explore technological support for their courses. The Prosperos suspect that the great virtual university in the sky will not exist in their lifetime (if at all), but that the development of viable technological resources to augment (and ultimately transform) instruction will be an additional burden to shoulder when many of them already feel over-extended.

In addition, "technology" is very institution specific. Few colleges and universities are blessed with the technological infrastructure situation we have at the Academy. Through e-mail and additional resources on a course Web page, I can easily provide that "contact" with faculty that is so desirable for student learning, knowing that our intranet provides easy access to my faculty students at their desktops. Not too long ago I visited a campus where technology was an increasing part of instruction but most students had to do assignments in cramped computer labs where there were at least three students standing in line for each terminal. This is why a centralized vision for the development of technology for instruction is so crucial. We should not be developing programs and practices that are at odds with our student-users' access.

To make progress, we need to vanquish the dualistic thinking that identifies technology as good and denigrates all traditional approaches. One experience of our Center is illustrative. When the CTE began, I wanted to publish a newsletter, but the Dean insisted that the Academy needed to go "paperless" and suggested I create an electronic newsletter. I did that for a year, but in the annual assessment faculty members commented that they would prefer traditional hard copy. Yes, they could download the electronic copy; but they claimed it was too easy to ignore it in the crush of daily imperatives. Coincidentally, the following year we had a new Dean who had no problem with the concept of a paper newsletter; and subsequently our annual assessment has indicated that it is the single feature of the CTE that touches each and every faculty member. It appears in their mailbox, and most keep it handy for a spare moment. It is portable; they do not need their computer to read it.

The Challenge

One of the best prescriptions I have encountered for applying technology to learning comes from the perspective of organizational reengineering. In 1996 Stahlke and Nyce posited a set of assumptions which "will require a rethinking of teaching and learning that can profoundly affect the roles and responsibilities of the student and the instructor, administrative support processes and calendars, and, in short, the entire structure and delivery of higher education" (p. 46). Their assumptions are relatively innocuous and would probably gain acceptance from most of the professoriate. Simply described, they would focus attention on the specific teaching-learning task and have the instructional event designed according to the nature of the teacher, learner, and content, using the methods and tools best suited to the learning environment. What they ask educators to abandon is the notion, implicit in higher education, that the default mode is the lecture hall and to instead employ a "research agenda in which we would apply the critical skills we associate with discipline-based research to the work we do as faculty members" (p. 47).

To illustrate this point, several years ago, I taught a developmental composition class. Since the students had varied ability levels, some of which were quite high and certainly seemed sufficient for the work in the freshman course they had failed, I hypothesized that they lacked an effective personal writing process. If that were true, the best form of instruction, I believed, would be a writing workshop in which I could monitor their writing processes and intervene as needed to strengthen their skills. I asked to teach in our technology classroom so that the students could write extensively and develop their processes.

I repeatedly elicited feedback from the students on their perceptions of their development as writers and the course methodology as a factor in their development. No one ever mentioned the use of technology. On the final course assessment, I specifically asked their opinion of using technology for writing instruction. Most students gave fairly neutral responses, but several specifically said that they believed that the amount of writing and the continual feedback on performance was what was most helpful; the technology was tangential. One student commented that we "could have done the same things if we had to write by hand." He was both correct and incorrect. Yes, I could have taught similarly without computers—and I have done so in the past—but I could not have gotten the same flexibility of revision and ease of writing. Having taught for some time without computers, I estimate that the development those students achieved in one semester would have required at least three semesters without the "tool" of the word processor. What the computers did was provide an opportunity for them to gain three times the benefit they would have received had the technology tools not been available.

Unless we see technology for instruction as one of many tools in our repertoire, and not as the focus, we will not effectively redesign instruction. If, however, we see it as a tool and simply replace the chalk with the mouse, we are doomed to the status quo—with very expensive teaching tools to assist us. Several of my colleagues discovered this in reverse. A few years ago, some members of our computer science department designed a course in computer systems using hypertext, multimedia, and hypermedia to provide a rich selection of tools to enhance student learning. They also used their computer science expertise to monitor student study times with the hypermedia tools. They discovered that the technology indeed enhanced the learning of the average and above average students but that the weak students were not performing well because they were not preparing for class. Despite the wealth of technology tools available, "the end result was a group of students performing poorly and learning little in the class" (Carver, Howard, and Lane, 1996, p. 24). These faculty members realized they needed to create an instructional methodology in the classroom that would impel the laggards to prepare for class, and they did so through active-learning, experiential activities. Technophiles often lament the limitations of faculty ability to create multimedia courseware as the central factor inhibiting the achievement of the "brave new world" of academe, but these colleagues were able to create every imaginable tool for students' use. Their experience affirms the fact that the design of the instructional event is the critical issue, and that design must be holistic to include all the components of the teaching and learning process. (See Chapter 4.)

Lessons Learned

An underlying belief about education is that we can learn from the experiences of others as well as from our own experiences. It is with this belief that lessons learned are offered.

Readiness is all. Higher education faculty members are not sheep. They prize their autonomy and are not easily persuaded to change time-honored pedagogies from which they themselves learned successfully. Most have seen educational fads come and go. Change will not happen in the sweeping fashion of industry or business. The best approach is to work with small groups of faculty members, whether within the department or college or at the institutional level, to examine the basic assumptions of instructional delivery. These small groups, in turn, can eventually create a ripple effect.

There is no "magic bullet." One of my army colleagues likes to say that faculty development is "a campaign, not a battle." And that is true of all change in higher education. One must beware of the cultural imperative toward the "quick fix." Because we are all conditioned by this longing for solutions, any institutional design for change should be built around small successes whenever possible. For example, in our required physical geography core course, students must know how to read a map, a skill they are taught in military science classes the preceding year. The geography course director, noting that valuable class time was spent reviewing map reading principles, has asked to have our multimedia developers work with an instructor to create a self-paced, map-reading tutorial for student use. The finished product will provide the geography faculty with a model for transforming their traditional instruction, and it will give us a model to show to others looking for solutions to instructional dilemmas.

Technology must not "wag the dog." As the computer scientists learned with their hypermedia course, the technology is only a tool and must be part of a sound instructional methodology. There must be educational leadership to assist faculty members in exploring issues involved in the use of technology and in examining the basic assumptions underlying time-honored pedagogies and traditional structures. Higher education faculty members think in terms of delivering instruction as it has always been done, and they want technology to make it better and easier. For there to be any transformation, technology must be subordinated to issues of overall instructional design.

Extrinsic incentives are helpful. It is usually said that extrinsic rewards should be minimized in motivating students, but it may be the reverse for faculty "students." Submitting to guidance within faculty development programs can be a threatening experience for faculty members; and to help people take the risk of engaging in group discussion of instructional re-design, a modest reward should always be offered, whether a free lunch, a small stipend, or a small grants program in support of technology implementation.

Faculty grief must be addressed. Change is not easy, and for every advance, there is some loss. Faculty members who become involved, however willingly, in any effort to change what has been traditional for them may exhibit expressions of grief because of the loss of what is familiar. Educational leaders must be sensitive to this and help colleagues deal with the stress of change rather than reacting negatively to these emotions. Faculty developers should also be prepared to help colleagues process negative feelings.

From these lessons, it should be clear that leadership is essential to this process. One of the problems with seeing the technology issue as one of machines and software is the focus on technical assistance for the faculty member, but the crucial issue is adequate educational leadership. The challenge of technology to time-honored pedagogies and traditional structures is also a challenge for leaders and faculty developers. Can the leadership come from the academic arena? If it does not, then there is little hope for positive change in teaching and learning with the assistance of technology.

Conclusion

Perhaps it is the speed of technological change over the past twenty years that makes technology highly attractive to some people and anathema to others. Or it may be the fact that faculty members in higher education have not simply spent their working lives in a specific context; they have spent their *entire lives* in a specific educational setting to which they have deep emotional attachments. We often view traditional structures and pedagogies—academic calendar, semesters or quarters, credit hours, lectures and discussion sections—less as the structure imposed on the teaching and learning process than as the process itself. Any threat of change in those structures and pedagogies can be a threat to who we are as well as what we do.

Is it any wonder that there would be resistance to the "brave new world" that purports to eliminate all of those things for the technological marvel of the virtual university? If institutions can help their faculty members view technology as the invited guest rather than the unwelcome stranger, the process of integration will be considerably facilitated. If, however, technology remains an intruder, its potential to improve and enhance student learning will be limited. One defends against intruders; one welcomes guests.

In addition, educational leadership is needed, lest we magnify the negatives in our traditional approaches to instruction rather than capitalize on the positives. For example, prior to current interest in technology, there was much discussion about improving student learning in large lecture classes. Techniques for peer and student-instructor interactivity were promoted to get students more actively engaged. Yet when technology was introduced into the lecture hall, it was not to promote this engagement but to enhance the presentation platform. Suddenly we were back to the one-way teaching that we already know is the downside of the lecture method. In promoting technology for instruction, we need to ensure that we are promoting good practices in teaching and learning.

We are already changing, so we might as well do it consciously. It may not be visible, but it is happening. For example, classes at West Point probably look as traditional today as they did five years ago; cadets go to classes at specified hours, and we emphasize student-teacher interaction during those class hours. But with a ubiquitous computing environment, the delivery of instruction transcends those class hours. Contact between cadets and faculty members can continue electronically throughout the evening study hours, and through automated systems instructors can determine what cadets find difficult in the homework before they arrive for class and plan instruction accordingly. As teaching and learning becomes less constrained by the class hour when students and instructor are in the same room, perceptions of learning will evolve. Eventually, perhaps the structures of credit hour and semester divisions will change as well, but we would do well to allow the evolution to proceed naturally. The wisdom of Prospero should not be sacrificed to the naïveté of Miranda.

References

Angelo, T. A. "From *Faculty* Development to *Academic* Development." *AAHE Bulletin,* 1994, *46* (10), 3–7.

Berger, J. "Screen Test for Main Street." *New York Times,* April 15, 1998, p. B1.

Bray, C. W. "Reflections: Productivity in Learning." *Wingspread Journal,* 1995, *17* (2), 3.

Carr, A. A., Jonassen, D. H., Litzinger, M. E., and Marra, R. M. "Good Ideas to Foment Educational Revolution: The Role of Systematic Change in Advancing Situated Learning, Constructivism, and Feminist Pedagogy." *Educational Technology,* Jan.–Feb. 1998, 5–15.

Carver, C. A., Howard, R. A., and Lane, W. "Active Student-Controlled Learning: Reaching the Weakest Students." *Liberal Education,* 1996, *82* (3), 24–29.

Chickering, A. W., and Ehrmann, S. C. "Implementing the Seven Principles: Technology as Lever." *AAHE Bulletin,* 1996, *49* (2), 3–6.

Dye, N. S. "Virtual College: The End of the Campus?" *Christian Science Monitor,* June 8, 1998, p. 11.

Ehrmann. S. C. "New Technology, Old Trap." *Educom Review,* 1995, *30* (5), 41–43.

Ewell, P. T. "Organizing for Learning: A New Imperative." *AAHE Bulletin,* Dec. 1997, *50* (4), 3–5.

Green, K. C. "The 1997 National Survey of Information Technology in Higher Education." [http://www.aahe.org]. 1997.

Monaghan, P. "U. of Washington Professors Decry Governor's Visions for Technology." *Chronicle of Higher Education,* June 19, 1998, p. A23.

Nantz, K. S., and Lundgren, T. D. "Lecturing with Technology." *College Teaching,* 1998, *46* (2), 53–56.

Neal, E. "Using Technology in Teaching: We Need to Exercise Healthy Skepticism." *Chronicle of Higher Education,* June 19, 1998, pp. B4–B5.

Noble, D. F. "Digital Diploma Mills: The Automation of Higher Education" [http://www.firstmonday.dk/issues/issues3/noble/index.html]. 1998.

Oberman, C. "The Need for Information Literacy: Now!" Paper presented at the annual conference of the Middle States Association of Colleges and Schools, Commission on Higher Education, Dec. 10, 1996.

Postman, N. "Making a Living, Making a Life: Technology Reconsidered." *College Board Review,* 1995, *176/177,* 8–13.

Stahlke, H.F.W., and Nyce, J. M. "Reengineering Higher Education: Reinventing Teaching and Learning." *CAUSE/EFFECT,* 1996, *19* (4), 44–51.

Twigg, C. A. "Superficial Thinking: The Productivity Paradox." *Educom Review,* 1995, *30* (5), 50–51.

Ullman, E. "Needed: Techies Who Know Shakespeare." *New York Times,* July 8, 1998, p. A21.

Williamson, S. R. "When Change Is the Only Constant: Liberal Education in the Age of Technology." *Educom Review,* 1996, *31* (6). Available at [http://www.educom.edu/web/pubs/review/reviewArticles/31639.html].

ANITA GANDOLFO is director of the Center for Teaching Excellence at the United States Military Academy, West Point, New York.

Thus far, the basis for the development of most instructional technology applications has been the process of systematic instructional design; however, the traditional model of systematic instructional design may no longer be appropriate for new technology tools.

Instructional Design for the New Technologies

Frank Gillespie

The excitement generated by new technologies has prompted many faculty members to seek assistance to enhance their teaching and improve the quality of learning opportunities for students. Never before have so many faculty members been so involved in using technology in their courses (Green, 1997). Never before have faculty developers and faculty support centers had such an opportunity to become so involved in fundamental matters relating to teaching and learning with such a highly motivated group of learners. In this chapter I compare the use of computer technology to support teaching and learning in the past with the educational opportunities now presented us. I also examine traditional processes employed to develop instructional applications and contrast them with design and development processes more appropriate for the new technologies.

New Possibilities

With new technologies, such as Internet-based or on-line courses, higher education faculty members can assume the roles of counselor, guide, and mentor as never before. With their new on-line courses they can spend *more time* planning and facilitating learning and developing higher order thinking skills and *less time* presenting content. With the technological capabilities available from on-line courses students can take more responsibility for their own learning than ever before. They can access information from more resources than just a single instructor or a single textbook, and they can collaborate with others within their class, across the country, or even around the world.

On-line courses are the latest in a long series of applications of information technology to support teaching and learning. They typically include all or a portion of the lessons, modules, lectures, readings, assignments, and other instructional materials that serve as the learning resources. These resources are available after being placed on a local area computer network or posted to the Internet, a global distribution of computer networks, through use of the World Wide Web, a document publishing and distribution system for the Internet.

Internet-based or on-line courses provide a medium of instruction enabling faculty members to extend teaching and learning opportunities. On-line instruction can combine features of synchronous and asynchronous communication, passive and active learning, and independent and group experiences. It may be supplemental or required by all students in a course, just one component of a course, or comprising the entire course. Common on-line instruction features such as chat rooms and electronic discussion groups allow learners to interact with their instructors, other students, the course content, and other resources and people around the world at a speed and in a manner never before possible. Many faculty members are intrigued by the capabilities of on-line instruction and are making efforts to convert some of their instruction to an on-line environment.

The new technologies, as exemplified by on-line instruction, have the potential to do wonderful things for teaching and learning and are perceived by many in a positive way. During seminars and classes on on-line course design, I have asked faculty members to identify what they hope to achieve by transforming their instruction with these technologies. They often comment about improving the quality of their instruction through better access to information and better contact with their students. They believe they will gain easier and earlier access to useful information and a better method for dissemination of this information to students. They expect the new technologies to provide more effective use of their time and students' time, and they hope to obtain an enhanced sense of community with and among students. These hopes may sound familiar to readers.

Development of Teaching and Learning with Technology

More than ten years ago such hopes were raised with the promises that computer technology would soon greatly influence teaching and learning (Bok, 1985; Chambers and Sprecher, 1980). By replacing or reducing the source and information transfer functions of teachers, microcomputer technology would soon allow more time for addressing students' special concerns, diagnosing learning problems, developing appropriate learning strategies, and monitoring the effects of instruction. Students would benefit by becoming more actively involved in the learning process, receiving immediate feedback about their performance, and being able to proceed at their own pace.

These were not the first promises about the potential effects of computer technology. Actually teaching and learning with and about computer technology has a history of nearly forty years, and promises of improvement with computer technology go back almost that far (Suppes, 1966). Since about 1960 there have actually been five distinct phases or trends in the use of computer technology for teaching and learning. Initially the computer was regarded just as a content to be taught, then as a means to enhance learning. Following the development and availability of inexpensive microcomputers in 1978, the computer began to be regarded for the first time as a personal support tool, then as a vehicle for hypertext and multimedia delivery, and finally as a powerful communication link between faculty and students.

After beginnings in the early 1960s with teaching the computer as content, the response judging and immediate feedback capabilities of the computer began to be employed to support the teaching of other types of content. Specialized instructional computing applications called computer assisted instruction (CAI), computer assisted learning (CAL), and elaborate mainframe based CAI systems such as PLATO and TICCIT had their beginnings in the mid 1960s. These systems eventually offered extensive collections of courseware that provided drill and practice, tutorial, simulation, and even problem solving exercises (Gagne, Wagner, and Rojas, 1981). PLATO, TICCIT and the IBM Coursewriter system also provided excellent examples of the application of systematic instructional design principles on a large scale. Most frequently development teams of content experts, computer programmers, and instructional designers used the steps of analysis, design, development, implementation, and evaluation to plan and deliver instructional materials on a large scale (Nievergelt, 1980). With the PLATO system, it took an estimated average of 100 hours to produce one hour of instructional material. By the mid to late 1970s over 10,000 kinds of course materials were available, and there is still an extensive library of such materials (NovaNet, 1998).

During the late 1970s the success of the personal microcomputer encouraged the development of tools and applications to enhance our productivity. The word processing, spreadsheet, graphics packages, database management, and telecommunications packages we use today had their beginnings about 1978 when the Apple II became available. The availability of these tools marked a departure from the need for faculty to employ systematic instructional design and programming skills to produce instructional applications. Faculty knowledgeable in the use of these tools could develop classroom exercises encouraging students to use the productivity tools to perform learning tasks. Improved versions of these tools continue in use today to support teaching and learning by enhancing our personal productivity and that of our students, both inside and outside the classroom.

Improvements in the capabilities of personal microcomputers during the mid-1980s encouraged the production of hypertext and multimedia educational programs. These programs were often CD-ROM based and presented course content with a variety of connections or links to examples using text, graphics, sound, animation, and video resources. They often included features for the presentation of questions or tasks and the judging of student responses as well as opportunities for students to explore and inquire. Some allowed students to apply concepts to problem solving or performing authentic tasks. Production of these types of programs usually involved teams of content experts, programmers, and instructional designers applying principles of systematic instructional design. Today there are probably over 5,000 educational titles available on CD-ROM and other types of computer-based media that provide examples of hypertext and multimedia educational programs (Armor Educational Video and CD-ROM catalog, 1998).

During the early 1990s the establishment of local and wide area networks and improved access to computers and communication resources encouraged the development of more new tools for connecting students and faculty. E-mail, bulletin boards, listserv discussion groups, and access to on-line resources such as syllabi, class materials, class notes files, cases, sample questions and answers, and sample student products became ubiquitous during this period. The availability of these resources and improved access to the Internet with links to local and global resources encouraged development and use of new teaching and learning models and activities. A major feature of these new communication resources is that they provide user-friendly opportunities for increased faculty-to-faculty, faculty-to-student, and student-to-student interactions while also providing extensive programming support or instructional design.

However, even with a history of nearly forty years, the actual impact of computer technology on instruction has not been that great. Until very recently the computer has been used mainly as an aid to faculty productivity and to support or enhance normal teaching activities. Until fairly recently there have been very few examples where computers have really changed how we teach or what is actually taught.

According to the 1997 Campus Computing Survey (Green, 1997) the most popular instructional technology applications in higher education today are e-mail, computer-generated presentations and handouts, and use of Internet resources. The 1997 survey reveals that nearly one-third of all college courses make use of e-mail and one-fourth use resources from the Internet. Use of these applications has increased from five to ten percent each year for the past three years. Use of CD-ROM and multimedia resources has also increased but at a rate of only about two percent per year.

New Tools and New Ways to Support Teaching and Learning

The promises of nearly forty years have not been realized, but progress has been made in the development of new tools and changes in the way we design and use computer applications to support teaching and learning. In the past the development of instructional computing applications required extensive programming support and the use of systematic instructional design principles. Use of modern productivity tools and telecommunication resources to support teaching and learning require neither, resulting in a shift in the way we can employ technology to support and enhance teaching and learning.

Previously, computer-based instructional applications such as CAI provided a structured teaching and learning environment that was under the direct control of the instructor. Short instructional modules on a few concepts within a single subject were the norm. The teacher and the CAI program, as an extension of the teacher, were dispensers of knowledge and supported the development of specific procedures or skills. In this one-way mode of instruction the student had few or no choices. Instruction occurred in small steps, and learners were required to demonstrate a specific level of knowledge or performance before they were allowed to continue. During each small instructional step the learners responded to stimuli that were constructed in such a way that correct responses were essentially assured (Markle, 1964). A sequence of instructional events or activities was presented in a lock step, linear manner; and all learners experienced essentially the same content and sequence of activities. The goals of the programs were the development and assessment of specific instructional or learner objectives and skills and methods that could be retained and used as necessary.

Unlike previous approaches to using instructional technology, which placed a high degree of structure or control on the learner, the new technology-based instructional applications provide an environment permitting more learner choices. Students can explore and be responsible for their learning. The learning environment is essentially unlimited, and exploration and learning from mistakes is accepted and even encouraged. Learners can proceed through a vast amount of content in an often unstructured or even random manner, and for two learners to have the same experiences would be highly unlikely. Allowing large jumps rather than small steps is the norm. Browsing, surfing the Web, and learning from mistakes are all possible and even encouraged with the new technologies. Thus, students become more engaged with the material. This seeming technological chaos can be used to develop problem solving skills and to practice critical thinking skills, rather than for the presentation of content.

The learning features available with the new teaching and learning tools represent a convergence in the five dimensions of instructional computing: (1) the computer as content to be taught, (2) a tool to support instruction, (3) a tool for personal productivity, (4) a means for hypertext and multimedia delivery, and (5) a device for communication between instructor and learner. These new teaching and learning opportunities represent a departure from the ways we traditionally think about employing technology to support teaching and learning. A comparison of the instructional capabilities of traditional and new teaching and learning tools is presented in Table 3.1.

This categorization fits the new paradigm proposed by Barr and Tagg (1995), whereby we move from a learning environment that is teacher directed to one that provides for more learner options. We can indeed do so, thus leaving behind us the teacher-controlled transfer of specific knowledge or skills to the learner.

Our On-Line Environment

In contrast to the realities of our educational past, the new paradigm and the capabilities of our on-line environment encourage options and choices for the learner in an unlimited learning environment. Learners proceed though a vast amount of content in an often apparently unstructured manner. Collaboration and cooperation are encouraged as are problem solving and critical thinking skills. All of this is a significant departure from the way we traditionally think about instruction. A comparison of the defining features of traditional and new teaching and learning approaches is presented in Table 3.2.

Higher education has begun to respond to the challenges of the new instructional paradigm in part by developing a strong technology component in its programs (O'Banion, 1997). Infrastructure is improving, and its critical importance is recognized. Faculty are now encouraged to develop on-line courses, and course development tools are becoming available. The examination of some of the current trends in higher education indicates that in itself just the availability

Table 3.1. Characteristics of Traditional and New Teaching and Learning Tools

Traditional Characteristics	New Characteristics
Teacher control	Learner options, choices
Structured content	Exploration of content
Errorless performance	Learn from errors
Small steps	Large jumps
Linear, limited branching	Linking
Local	Global
Transfer knowledge, specific skills	Learn problem solving
Teach procedures	Practice critical thinking skills
Control the learner	Empower the learner

Table 3.2. Comparisons of Traditional and New Paradigm Approaches

Traditional Approaches to Instruction	The New Paradigm
Teacher-directed	Learner-centered
Didactic teaching	Student exploration
Short blocks of instruction on a single subject	Extended blocks of multidisciplinary instruction
Passive or one-way modes of instruction	Active and interactive modes of instruction
Individual, competitive work	Collaborative, cooperative work
Teacher as knowledge dispenser	Teacher as facilitator or guide
Ability grouping	Heterogeneous grouping
Assessment of knowledge, specific skills	Performance-based assessment

of new technology is playing a significant role in encouraging use. Some new aspects of on-line instruction are directed to improving learning by reducing time, labor, or costs. Others provide new or more convenient ways to deliver instruction or increase or improve educational access. Still others are directed to exploring the potential that technology has for improving the quality of teaching and learning. The most attractive of these models to individual faculty members are those that involve improvements in the quality of their individual teaching and the learning of the specific students in their classes. Let us return to the earlier hopes expressed about technology and instruction.

By using the new technologies faculty members can address teaching and learning issues in several ways. They can enhance quality by enabling students to take more active roles in the learning process. They can present their course in ways that recognize and use a variety of learning styles. They can make available a greater array of resources for their students to use both inside and outside the classroom. They can provide increased opportunities for interactions between and among their students. Perhaps most importantly, they can provide experiences that promote the development of higher-order cognitive skills rather then the transfer of content.

Typical first time instructional uses of technology by faculty members include using computer-driven projection devices, using technology to teach specific topics, and introducing e-mail into a course (Gilbert, 1996). In spite of the potential of the new technology, most faculty members continue to present content and to test and evaluate the attainment of that content. In so doing, they are failing to meet the challenges presented by the new paradigm and the opportunities presented by the new technologies and are just transferring forms of instruction already used in the classroom to the computer (Alexander, 1995). As so often happens, we first use a new technology in old ways. Consideration of the instructional design process can enhance our understanding of how a technology tool is appropriately used to support teaching and learning.

Systematic Instructional Design

The development of a teaching-learning system employing technology represents a considerable investment in time and effort. Traditionally development has been enhanced by a complex systematic process resulting in a description of the sequence, relationship, and interaction of components of the teaching-learning system. A number of strategies have been suggested to facilitate the development of teaching and learning systems.

Thus far, the basis for the development of most instructional technology applications has been the process of systematic instructional design. This process is directed to creating instructional plans that, if followed, will lead the student to the achievement of specific learning objectives. Systematic instructional design is largely a matter of organizing learning events in some order determined by the teacher or the instructional designer (Smith, 1993), and the outcome is a highly structured lesson or course. The process is generally understood as consisting of five distinct stages—analysis, design, development, implementation and evaluation.

Analysis. The analysis phase is the foundation for all other phases. Instructional needs and learner characteristics are examined, and goals and purposes are defined. The major focus of the analysis stage is to identify what is needed or what we want to do differently. Typical questions asked during the analysis include: where are the students having difficulty? what knowledge, skills and attitudes do they have? and what knowledge and skills do they need? Possible sources of data for answering these questions include examining tests to determine student misconceptions, discussing perceptions of student difficulties with other students and colleagues, and testing or observing students' current knowledge in comparison with what they should know or demonstrate at the completion of the instruction. The results of the analysis phase are the identification of instructional needs, the determination of learner characteristics, and the development of program goals and purposes.

Design. In the design phase the results from the analysis are employed to plan strategies for the actual development and delivery of the instructional program. Learner objectives and assessment measures are developed; and instructional content, processes, and resources are specified. Design involves answering fundamental questions about what the students will learn, how they will demonstrate what they have learned, and how the learning will occur. The first two of these questions are answered by specifying all learner objectives and then creating test items or alternative assessment techniques corresponding to each learner objective. The third question is answered by considering the structure and organization of content, the processes and activities appropriate for achieving the learning objectives, and the resources appropriate for the objectives and content being addressed. This consideration can be facilitated by constructing a concept map of the material, determining the best way to sequence the content, specifying instructional processes appropriate for achieving the objectives, and identifying media and other instructional resources appropriate for concretely conveying the content involved. Decisions relating to objectives, instructional content, processes, and resources can be facilitated by researching what objectives, strategies, and resources are appropriate; conducting interviews or focus groups with students; and discussing options with colleagues. Costs, time, effort, and legality are also considered during the design phase.

Development, Implementation, and Evaluation. The three final phases involve making all preparations for the project, actually conducting the project, and assessing effectiveness and efficiency. During the development phase results from the analysis and design phases are used to generate all instructional plans and materials, develop or acquire needed hardware, software or media, and produce support documentation. The implementation phase is concerned with the actual delivery of the instructional system and the achievement of the learner objectives. The evaluation phase measures the effectiveness and efficiency of the total instructional system and the individual analysis, design, development, and implementation phases. The evaluation phase actually occurs throughout the entire instructional design process and provides data for decisions about system improvement, continuation, modification, or termination. For the past thirty years this process has been used for developing instructional applications of technology.

The New Model of Instructional Design

However, the traditional model of systematic instructional design may no longer be appropriate for new technology tools because it requires the specification of precise levels of content and learning objectives and is based on the teacher as content expert and controller of student learning. The capabilities of the new technologies negate the need for a content expert as the controller of learning. When confronted with an instructional design task, faculty members in this traditional role tend to "overspecify" and produce a product that emphasizes lower order cognitive tasks and levels of learning. These efforts often result in a technology-based teaching and learning environment that emphasizes the transfer, acquisition, and retaining of knowledge (Duchastel, 1997). Faculty members should now reject the systematic instructional design process and instead ask themselves two questions:

What do I want to do differently?
How can I use the new tools to accomplish what I want?

Because of the availability of the new technologies and because knowledge and information are now easily available in so many forms, the transmission of knowledge and assessing the degree to which knowledge has been acquired by an individual student should no longer be the main focus of instruction. Efforts spent transferring lecture notes to on-line courses and presentation graphic programs are of questionable value, as are on-line quizzes and other forms of interactive assessment. The focus in using the new technologies should instead be on helping learners become skilled at finding and accessing appropriate information, evaluating it critically, using it to solve problems, and presenting the results of their learning experience.

In response to the question "what do I want to do differently?" faculty members should move from a focus on low level cognitive tasks to the development of higher-level thinking skills. Angelo and Cross (1993) in their Teaching Goals Inventory present eight higher-order thinking skills (pp. 20–21). These skills encourage the development of an ability to apply principles and generalizations already learned to new situations, analytic skills, problem solving skills, drawing reasonable inferences from observations, synthesizing and integrating information and ideas, thinking holistically, thinking creatively, and being able to distinguish fact from opinion. The new technologies provide unlimited opportunities for addressing these thinking skills, which can also provide the basis for how we can use the new technologies to support our teaching and learning in new ways.

When planning an on-line experience the faculty member should first identify a statement of purpose for the experience. This statement provides a direction and focus for all further development and can be constructed by considering the following questions:

Who are the learners?
What higher-level thinking skill will the learners address?
What areas of knowledge will be explored?
What learner tasks will facilitate the exploration of this knowledge?
What evidence of higher-level thinking will the learners provide?

By responding to these questions the faculty member is able to identify a high level thinking skill and an area of knowledge for a specific group of learners. In addition, the faculty member is able to describe tasks the learners could perform in order to explore the content and describe what evidence of higher-level thinking should be provided. A statement of purpose will also stimulate involvement on the part of the learner by describing the performance of specific high level tasks to be communicated and shared with the instructor and other students.

As an example, let us take the sixth higher order teaching skill identified by Angelo and Cross—the ability to synthesize and integrate information and ideas—and develop it as a learning goal with the outlines of a new instructional design approach. While this is a goal that most faculty members would agree is essential and one that they try to address nearly all the time, many would have difficulty describing which of their specific teaching and learning activities actually contribute to it. By specifying this goal as the major purpose of a particular instructional activity and using the capabilities of the new technologies, a faculty member could develop learning tasks that direct learners to explore resources on the Internet relating to an area of knowledge and develop a personalized interpretation of what they discovered. Specification of the area of knowledge involved would only have to be made in very general terms, such as an exploration of *theories of learning*. The students would be encouraged to explore the Internet in whatever way and using as many resources relating to *theories of learning* as they wish.

A description of the actual tasks to be performed by the learner could be facilitated by employing specific cognitive strategies. West, Farmer, and Wolff (1991) present several cognitive strategies that could have direct application to learning tasks involving the new technologies. The actual learning tasks performed would consist of applying cognitive strategies associated with developing schemata, the patterns or structures in which our minds store knowledge, while exploring specific areas of knowledge with the Internet. The cognitive strategies that would have value to students while they explore the Web and the Internet are the strategies of chunking, frames, and concept maps.

Chunking is a preparatory cognitive strategy concerned with ordering, classifying, or arranging a specific body of content. Chunking strategies are of two major types and include linear or spatial strategies and classification strategies. With linear or spatial strategies the learner examines the concrete structure of a body of content, such as a painting or a map, and constructs an organization for it. With other linear strategies the learner can use time as the organizer to describe a sequence of events, or specific procedures, or some logical steps to organize the content. Classification types of chunking include those techniques that use taxonomies, typologies, or multipurpose sorting methods to organize content. Taxonomies are based on some logical rules or laws governing interrelationships. Typologies use some structural feature for organization, such as size, shape, color, or texture. Multipurpose sorting techniques organize content on the basis of relationships such as cause and effect, similarities and differences, form and function, and advantages and disadvantages.

The steps in the learning task relating to chunking that the learners in this example would follow would be to explore several resources of the Internet concerned with *theories of learning.* They would analyze the chunking strategies used in the content presented by the Internet resources they examined. They would describe the chunking strategies used and determine appropriate strategies for rechunking all the content that had been explored. They would emphasize their new chunking strategy in describing the content they had explored.

The cognitive strategy of frames involves the construction of a matrix or grid of the concepts, categories, or relationships that exist between two or more related bodies of content. Frame construction begins with an examination of the content areas to identify relationships between major ideas and concepts, previously identified by employing chunking strategies. Common features that define the relationships are arranged in a matrix, and individual cells depicting the similarities and differences between the content areas are described. With the example relating to *theories of learning,* relationships between behaviorist and cognitive theories of learning could be described in terms of a matrix or frame.

A third type of cognitive strategy is the concept map, which is an arrangement of concepts and relationships into a visual display or model. Major concepts within a specific content area are identified, lines are drawn between associated concepts, and relationships are named. A concept map could be constructed for a specific area of content, such as behaviorism, or several related areas within the larger content area of *theories of learning.*

Evidence of the completion of specific learning tasks would be the sharing of the examples of chunking, frames, or concept maps developed by the learners. The completed products and intermediate steps leading to the final product would be shared with an instructor and other learners by using the communication capabilities of the Internet and resources available in an online course. Feedback, clarification, and suggestions for improvements would contribute to the development of higher order cognitive processes.

Thus, the instructional design process appropriate for using the new technologies now emerges as a process based on teacher awareness of content resources available to students and consisting of identifying higher-order thinking skills to be explored, identifying areas of exploration in general terms, describing learning tasks incorporating cognitive strategies, and sharing evidence of completion of learning tasks with others.

Challenges of the New Instructional Design Process

Encouraging learners to become more involved with the content at a higher level and to collaborate with other learners requires several changes in how we regard teachers and content, learners, and faculty developers.

Teachers will need to assume a greater role as planners, designers, guides, mentors, and facilitators and must be willing to relinquish their role as providers of content. They will need to be technologically literate and use the new technology in all aspects of their professional work as well as in support of teaching and learning. In their involvement with their area of content expertise they will need to focus on the higher-order cognitive processes and the development of thinking skills and cognitive strategies. Transfer of knowledge and information will not be sufficient. The Internet will continue to grow and provide ever greater access to more and more information and knowledge. The content expert will need to help learners develop skills in organizing and making meaningful use of this knowledge.

Learners will need to assume greater responsibility for their own learning and be more willing to communicate and share the results of their explorations with others. They will need to practice specific cognitive skills and develop the skills necessary for cooperation and collaboration with others. They will need to be familiar with how to use the tools of the new technology to explore and investigate and how to share the results of their explorations with others. Skills in writing and maintaining journals documenting the completion of learning tasks will be essential.

Because many of these capabilities will be unfamiliar to faculty members and learners there will be a need for faculty to work closely with faculty development personnel in the design of appropriate learning tasks utilizing cognitive strategies. Faculty development personnel will also need to assist faculty members in the difficult task of changing their teaching behaviors and moving from a teacher centered to a student centered form of learning. Faculty members will need to be prepared for some of the resistance they will encounter from students as movement is made toward a learner centered experience. Faculty development personnel will also need to assist faculty members in obtaining more support for the development of new instructional models and securing some rewards or recognition for their efforts. Integration of the new technologies into existing programs is a formidable task, and faculty members' efforts can be enhanced by faculty development personnel helping them to document and maintain records and communicate results to other faculty members and administrators.

Conclusion

Over the next decade instructional technology will continue to provide enhanced opportunities for interaction between the teacher and learner and global access to knowledge and information. The incorporation of text, audio, graphics, animation, and video into all types of teaching and learning activities for individuals and groups will become commonplace. "Learning on demand" will be available to all students where they live, work, or study. These changes require us to rethink our design of instruction.

These new opportunities present serious challenges for change in the academy, but the biggest challenge will continue to be about how higher education can identify and work on issues of common concern to all of us. We must work together to examine our teaching, research, and service missions and determine what we need or want to accomplish with the new technologies. Only then should we begin to identify strategies where the new technologies have the potential to help us achieve our shared goals. Before we can apply comprehensive design strategies to address shared goals we must experiment, assess the effects of our individual experiences with the new technologies, and share what we discover. The results of our explorations ultimately should be used to help us select, design, implement, and support new technology strategies that can finally influence how our students learn and how we teach.

In the meantime, until we learn how to work together, we can explore how to use the new technology tools in our own teaching and learning and in our everyday work. We can cooperate with each other in learning about and using the new technologies. We can show others how we use information technology to enhance our teaching and learning. We can provide many more examples and models. We can recognize, reward, and support adopters of technology. We can encourage access to technology for everyone who wants it. We can examine the effects of technology on the teaching and learning of others and develop realistic plans for incorporating technology into our own teaching and learning.

The technology revolution in education will continue to be about access to information and ways of sharing this information, but hopefully also about what we can do with the information once it has been accessed and shared.

References

Alexander, S. "Teaching and Learning on the World Wide Web." Paper presented at AusWeb95, the first Australian World Wide Web conference, Ballina, New South Wales, Australia, April 30–May 2, 1995. Available at [http://www.iim.uts.edu.au/about/SAMC.html]. July 1998.

Angelo, T., and Cross, K. P. Classroom Assessment Techniques: A Handbook for College Teachers. (2nd ed.) San Francisco: Jossey-Bass, 1993.

Armor Educational Video and CD-ROM Catalog. [http://www.aenterprises.com/]. Aug. 1998.

Barr, R., and Tagg, J. "From Teaching to Learning: A New Paradigm for Undergraduate Education." *Change,* 1995, *27* (6), 13–17.

Bok, D. "Looking into Education's High-Tech Future." *Harvard Magazine,* 1985, *87* (5), 30–32.

Chambers, J. A., and Sprecher, J. W. "Computer Assisted Instruction: Current Trends and Critical Issues." *Communications of the ACM,* 1980, *2* (6), 332–335.

Duchastel, P. "A Web-Based Model for University Education." *Journal of Educational Technology Systems,* 1997, *25* (3), 221–228.

Gagne, R., Wagner, W., and Rojas, A. "Planning and Authoring Computer-Assisted Instruction Lessons." *Educational Technology,* 1981, 17–20.

Gilbert, S. W. "Making the Most of a Slow Revolution." *Change,* 1996, *28* (2), 10.

Green, K. C. "The 1997 National Survey of Information Technology in Higher Education, Campus Computing Project." [http://ericir.syr.edu/Projects/ Campus_computing/index.html]. 1997.

Markle, S. M. *Good Frames and Bad: A Grammar on Frame Writing.* New York: Wiley, 1964.

Nievergelt, J. "A Pragmatic Introduction to Courseware Design." *Computer,* 1980, *13* (9), 7–14.

"NovaNet.® A registered service mark of NovaNET Learning, Inc., Tucson, Ariz." [http://www.novanet.com]. Aug. 1998.

O'Banion, T. *A Learning College for the 21st Century.* Phoenix: Oryx Press, 1997.

Smith, P. L., and Ragan, T. J. *Instructional Design.* New York: Macmillan, 1993.

Suppes, P. "The Use of Computers in Education." *Scientific American,* 1966, *215,* 206.

West, C. K., Farmer, J. A., and Wolff, P. M. *Instructional Design: Implications for Cognitive Science.* Needham Heights, Mass.: Allyn & Bacon, 1991.

FRANK GILLESPIE is coordinator for instructional support in the Office of Instructional Support and Development, The University of Georgia, Athens, Georgia.

We do not yet know enough about on-line groups and environments to say that if you build this, a sense of community will come. Experiences in virtual environments are like snowflakes: no two are ever alike.

Community On-Line: New Professional Environments for Higher Education

Tony Di Petta

Imagine that you are asked to join an international group doing innovative work in your field of study. Now imagine that you know none of these persons and that you will never meet them face-to-face, hear their voices, or share a meal. You will collaborate with these invisible colleagues from your home or office, sending and receiving computer messages. Can you imagine that in such circumstances you would develop a sense of camaraderie and personal attachment to these people? Would you ever describe such an environment as a community?

For over two years I have worked in just such a technologically generated environment and have also played, studied, and developed personal friendships in that environment. I am not alone in this. According to the New York–based research firm *Find/SVP,* in 1998 more than 11 million people in North America used networked communication and information technologies to work and socialize in virtual meeting places that exist only in the vacuum of cyberspace.

As a child of the 1960s growing up in a small town by Lake Erie I developed strong attachments to people, places, and experiences that defined community for me. Community meant proximity or closeness, a sense of comfort and familiarity with my environment, and shared experience. These experiences gave me a sense of connectedness and social belonging that infused my personal and professional sense of values, behavior, and expectations.

As I enter middle age, both physically and professionally, I realize I have always been drawn to places or groups characterized by this strong sense of community. I should not have been surprised, then, to find that I associate

NEW DIRECTIONS FOR TEACHING AND LEARNING, no. 76, Winter 1998 © Jossey-Bass Publishers similar feelings with the technologically mediated virtual groups of which I have been a member. In the on-line environments of my professional life in the 1990s a "virtual community" elicits some of the same feelings associated with the community relationships of my youth.

Feeling part of a professional community gives meaning to the work I do in higher education. As higher education changes dramatically in response to public calls for accountability, economic realities, and the rapid spread of technology, faculty need new ways of working together to prepare for and shape their professional futures. Community as an ideal combined with computer mediated communication technology can help redefine teaching, learning, research, service, and professional development in higher education. In this chapter I will talk about the nature of community, virtual community, and the relevance of the two to faculty in higher education.

Community in the Age of Information

While certainly not a new word, *community* has become an Information Age buzzword, and the term is generally associated with individuals coming together to share experiences, interests, or goals. What is it about the concept of community that people find so appealing? M. Scott Peck, psychologist and author, says that community is more than an instinctive human need for association. In *The Different Drum* (1987), he argued, "Human beings have often been referred to as social animals. But we are not yet community creatures. We are impelled to relate to each other for our survival. But we do not as yet relate with the inclusivity, realism, self-awareness, vulnerability, commitment, openness, freedom, equality, and love of genuine community. It is clearly no longer enough to be simply social animals, babbling together at cocktail parties and brawling with each other in business and over boundaries. It is our task—our essential, central, crucial task—to transform ourselves from mere social creatures into community creatures" (p. 165). In this Information Age, even with all of our comforts and scientific and technological advancements, we still feel the need for something more. There is a growing belief that returning to and strengthening community, in a traditional sense of shared values, association, and interpersonal commitment, can relieve the isolation and lack of connection felt by individuals in postmodern society. In a culture where communication technology can almost instantaneously link us together, anywhere in the world, people can still feel alienated and long to be a part of something greater than themselves.

It may seem paradoxical that a technology that involves sitting alone in front of a display screen can meet some aspect of our human need for community. However, since its inception in the early 1970s, computer mediated communication (CMC) technology has been doing just that. Howard Rheingold (1993), an early popularist of computer-based discussion groups, says that electronic environments for group discussion are a new form of community—*virtual community*. He believes these *virtual* or *on-line communities* have developed in response to people feeling a "Hunger for community that has followed the disintegration of traditional communities around the world."

It is a human imperative to strive for community as an ideal which is more about the human spirit than anything else. Even in its virtual form community is an expression of our deep desire for belonging and need to define ourselves through our connections with others.

Defining Community

Defining community is difficult because people understand it differently. I have been referring to community as a social or spiritual connection which is "felt" among individuals. Others may emphasize different conditions associated with the concept. A sense of place or geographic proximity, an interdependence among members, shared values or purposes, and a common system of organization or governance have all been said to contribute to a feeling of community.

Thomas Sergiovanni (1993), who has done extensive work on community-building in schools, defined a community as a "collection of individuals who are bonded together by natural will and who are together binded to a set of shared ideas and ideals" (p. xvi). He explained that community does not evolve passively among people who interact; instead, people seek membership in a group based on meanings they hold about what is important.

In North America we play organized sports, socialize in clubs, and work together in a variety of functionally arranged groups. Often these groups share a common vision or purpose, and they are structured to facilitate communication and interaction in order to reach specific goals. Should we call these groups communities?

Shared vision and communication are two of the essential conditions of any definition of community. Peter Senge (1990), writing from an organizational leadership perspective, describes shared vision as the "pictures or images that people carry around in their heads and hearts" (p. 206). He says that shared images provide an organization with a sense of commonality, purpose, and cohesion needed to reach its goals by linking people in common caring. This empowers them with a feeling of community through a belief that they are engaged and connected in a worthwhile activity.

Communication is another key component of community because the words bring people closer together through shared understanding. Without communication we cannot share our hopes, fears, expectations, or dreams with others. And without communication we cannot develop the connections and closeness that move a group from a task orientation to a community orientation.

If shared vision and communication are enough to define a group as a community, then the teams and organizational groups to which we all belong should be called communities. Sergiovanni (1993) argues, however, that organizations cannot be equated with communities. He says that at their core communities and organizations are different. Communities are socially arranged around relationships and values while organizations tend to tie people together for specific purposes and goals. The former relationships rely on personal interconnections based on deeply held personal values and beliefs, while the latter relationships are based on instrumental and pragmatic arrangements. I would add that the focus of one is cooperation, and the focus of the other is collaboration. In organizations people cooperate, working to meet goals established to benefit the organization first. In a community people collaborate, sharing leadership and responsibility for shaping their individual and collective goals. Community then evokes a sense of "we-ness" that develops as experiences and values are shaped and shared over time. It also implies a process of shared doing, or a commitment to *doing with* others rather than going it alone. It is this *sharing* of selves and purposes that builds meaningful relationships and traditions that define and sustain the members of a community.

When sharing really means that individual differences are subjugated to assimilation and uniformity, however, community can be problematic. Philosopher Lynda Stone (1996) states that defining community on the basis of cultural or intellectual conformity runs counter to Western traditions of individualism, rationality, and freedom of choice. Similarly Iris Young (1990) argues that defining community in these narrow or restrictive terms tends to privilege sameness over difference and immediacy over mediation. The result is that differences within groups are suppressed, and individuals who may be different are excluded from membership. These views on the relationship of individuality and conformity in community resonate with Gozdz's (1993) metaphor for Peck's view of community as a salad composed of individual ingredients but making something greater than the sum of the parts.

If organizations cannot be defined as communities and shared vision and communication are insufficient to define groups as communities, then something else is needed. Perhaps it is a purpose or a cause to rally around. We have all seen how in times of crisis individuals can band together as a community to help each other. It may be that a sense of community was already present in the group and only needed a crisis or struggle to bring it out. Just as likely, groups may need a crisis to help them focus on their commonality and provide a common purpose for collective action. Banding together in common caring is a necessary part of transforming a collection of individuals sharing interests into the more complex social arrangement of supportive relationships and shared vision that we consider a community.

Community has traditionally been used to categorize or describe a set of representative characteristics, usually cultural and geographic, that define a group. We can for example talk of the Italian community of Little Italy or the Cajun community of New Orleans. More and more, however, community is thought of in a participatory and democratic way rather than as a set of descriptions. People choose to belong to a community and negotiate and renegotiate their conditions of membership. This is especially true in the on-line or virtual communities of which I have been a member. Viewed in this way community is a process, a transformative process of becoming who we individually and collectively want to be. In the final analysis community is a choice that people make and then struggle to achieve or maintain.

Perspectives on Community in Organizations and Professional Groups

In general, organizations and professional groups interpret community in their own way. From an organizational perspective any group of people that shares common interests—personal, cultural, or professional—can be called a community. The focus of the organizational view is defining and achieving organizational goals, which is a function of organizational survival. As Pinchot (1996) says, developing a community feeling within an organization is a necessary part of effective organizational leadership. In the literature of organizational management and leadership the promotion of a sense of community is a common strategy for building a successful organization. Managers recognize that a feeling of community adds to employee and customer satisfaction. A feeling of community can also help reduce employee turnover and increase productivity.

Professional groups also promote the idea of community. Professional networks are defined as groups of individuals sharing the same profession and meeting to discuss professional issues, and they are known as *professional communities*. Community for professional groups implies mutual benefit and professional development. Professionals, especially in the education sector, suggest that a sense of community motivates them, promotes sharing of subject-matter knowledge, builds professional confidence, and contributes to improved practice and increased public confidence (Lieberman and Grolnick, 1996).

Pinchot (1996) says that organizations should promote a sense of community. It is a phenomenon that can be created, and in community there is strength for both individuals and their organizations. Organizational representations of community tend, in my view however, to stress teamwork over interpersonal relationships and to exploit the social aspects and mythology of community for instrumental purposes related to the bottom line. Professional groups stress a sense of community that benefits individuals as part of a collective. Representations of professional community, unlike organizational representations of community, evoke for me a feeling that individual experience and expertise are valued and that we are bound together as a group of individuals for the purpose of improving our professional practice. The pace, structure, and demands of our workaday lives, however, often limit opportunities for participating in professional development activities or peer interactions that promote a sense of professional community.

Professional Community in Higher Education

In higher education we are members of many organizational and social groups but few communities. Organizational groups are found at the level of faculty associations, departments, and areas of study. We understand ourselves to be a specific part of a larger group of academics and educators to whom we feel a professional connection. We work with our students in class or with peers conducting research in organizational groups, and sometimes these groups feel like professional communities of learning or inquiry. It is when our work groups develop characteristics of more socially defined professional communities that the greatest benefits of community accrue.

When we feel part of a professional community, we relate on the basis of something more than the need for order or achievement. We feel an intimacy with other scholars because we know that we share the same purposes and values concerning our scholarship and our discipline. The relationship is more than practical; it is a relationship in which people are connected because of a shared vision of education or perhaps a shared love of a discipline. This is more than an agreement to work together organizationally.

What many are realizing is that the CMC technology of the Information Age can facilitate the interaction needed to replicate some aspects of professional community feeling within groups. The adoption of this technology has contributed to a new social phenomenon known as the virtual, or on-line, community. Virtual environments for group work and communication can provide greater access to, and flexibility in, professional association and development for faculty in higher education. They contribute to a sense of professional community by providing new ways and means for faculty members to work with one another.

Virtual Communities

Virtual, or on-line, communities, descriptors of a new kind of technologically mediated social environment, link people together in virtual meeting places that exist neither here where I am, nor there where you are, but somewhere else between us in cyberspace. People define and build these virtual places with their words, in a process of sustained text-based discussion through their computers.

Are these virtual places communities? They feel like it at times. In on-line discussion groups you meet new people and confront new ideas. In the boundaryless world of cyberspace, where millions of people are communicating and presenting their particular views and interpretations of the world, finding a group of like-minded individuals who share their particular interests or ideas provides a community feeling like coming home.

People and organizations, however, tend to interpret and represent virtual community differently just as they do with more traditional concepts of community. Media and marketing professionals see virtual communities as on-line special interest groups or new audiences for advertising. Business groups interpret on-line community as a means of improving organizational morale, corporate leadership, and employee productivity. Many of the tenants of on-line communities, however (myself included), see these technologically mediated environments as a new form of social and professional community. That is, we view our on-line meeting spaces and the people who share these environments with us as neighborhoods of our personal and professional lives.

Sometimes, under conditions that still remain largely undefined, virtual neighborhoods can feel as personal and real as the physical neighborhoods in which we live and work. In fact, researchers who studied early communications networks established in large organizations like IBM report that employees participating in virtual communities often felt closer to these distant colleagues than they did to co-workers in the same building or office (Paulsen, 1992).

The first time that I became aware that CMC technology could trigger feelings of community was when I hosted a series of on-line discussion forums for higher education professionals interested in designing and implementing on-line courses at their institutions. Over a hundred university and college instructors from Europe, Australia, South America, Canada, and the United States, whose disciplines ranged from liberal arts to applied sciences and technology, gathered electronically in a virtual discussion space to share experiences and ideas. For eight weeks, while these forums were ongoing, I sat daily in front of my computer screen for two or three hours and read or posted messages. The forums were a practical means of professional development for all of us. We mentored each other, offered words of encouragement, and worked together to improve practice; and we developed a strong sense of shared purpose. But I did not develop a sense of professional or social community with this group, and I doubt that anyone else did either. Perhaps this was because of the limited amount of time that was available for social discussion or interaction. Perhaps we lacked a sense of crisis or struggle that might have been provided by a deadline or some other sense of urgency. I did, however, develop a sense of professional and social community with the members of the technical team that worked behind the scenes to make the forums possible.

As a group of six colleagues working together, we struggled together to plan and implement an on-line environment and a process for professional development opportunity. We brainstormed, argued about the best way to do things, and shared jokes and war stories in our own on-line space. Over the eight weeks that virtual space became a second home for us, and the bond continues even though the forums have ended. It was first established in our virtual space, but it was reinforced when we met face to face, which felt like a reunion for a group of old friends.

Virtual communities of professional or social interest are creating a myriad of new social groupings that were not possible before. Barriers of time and distance that can limit professional association are largely removed by meeting in these virtual spaces. Nicholas Negroponte (1995), writing on the cultural impact of computer technology, observed that computer technology is no longer about computers or how to use them, rather it is about living. But where did all this community building technology come from, and where will it lead?

A Brief History of Community Technology

People create meaning through the sharing of stories, which help us make sense of the world around us. One of the stories that helped me make sense of computer communication technology as a community-building tool is that of the "talking heads." In the politically turbulent period of the early 1960s, when world political leaders were struggling with the Cuban Missile Crisis, the President of the United States wanted to be able to quickly and efficiently contact foreign heads of state. In order to accomplish this, the story goes, a room in the White House was set up with teletype machines connected through telephone lines to teletypes in similar rooms in a number of foreign capitals. Directly above each teletype machine was placed a picture of the foreign head of state to which the teletype linked the President. Whenever a message came through on one of the teletype terminals, it seemed as if that particular head of state was talking; and so the terminals became known as the talking heads. The talking heads represented a new application of communication technology for linking groups of people together asynchronously.

Whether the talking heads story is historically accurate or not is unimportant. What matters is that the desire of the United States government to develop an international communication system that would guarantee delivery of military, government, and research information to critical centers in case of war or other emergency represents the impetus for what we now call the Internet or the Information Superhighway—the birthplace of on-line discussion groups and newsgroups. In these virtual environments the technology functions almost like a partner in the dialogue by facilitating the information flow and enabling the interactive communication that defines these groups as virtual communities.

In the early 1990s futurists such as Rheingold (1993) and Hiltz and Turoff (1993) predicted that these on-line communities would experience enormous growth as rich new environments for human connection and interaction. The predictions are coming true and nowhere is the spread of on-line environments more rapid or the potential for creating rich new human interaction greater than in higher education.

On-Line Environments in Higher Education

In higher education, on-line environments for teaching and learning are promoted as a way of providing flexible access and addressing the changing needs of students in a technologically sophisticated world. That this technology will change how we relate to and work with students and each other is undeniable.

Windschitl (1998) noted that what educators liked best about the networked communication and information technology was the increased access to people and resources. I have taught in a number of on-line environments and have marveled at the level of student participation and interaction. I have also worked with colleagues on line and have developed friendships and associations in these environments that make me feel part of an international professional community of higher education. I would have had very limited access to these colleagues or opportunities without the technology that made it possible to collaborate at a distance.

On-line environments in higher education are also viewed as a way of providing increased access to professional development opportunities for faculty and staff. Traditional delivery methods for professional development in higher education are associated with a variety of costs. Getting together with colleagues in face-to-face settings often involves travel and housing costs and finding time within already busy professional schedules. These considerations can make professional development an expensive proposition for faculty and institutions. As this volume suggests, the technology offers us ways of extending faculty development opportunities beyond the traditional. Nonetheless, virtual environments for faculty development and association are not without their own unique problems or costs.

Issues of Virtual Communities in Higher Education

Creating the infrastructure to develop and support virtual work environments for faculty, staff, and students is an expensive and complicated undertaking. Along with specialized hardware and software, skilled technological and administrative personnel are needed to build and maintain these systems. However, the problems and issues most associated with attempts to create on-line communities in higher education are not related to infrastructure. Rather they are related to access and a need to carefully map the landscape of the on-line frontier before trying to establish professional communities there.

For many faculty members access to on-line environments is affected by a variety of factors including the cost of buying the necessary equipment, the need for computers at home and work, prerequisite skills, and finding the time to explore these virtual environments so as to make them inhabitable. Further complicating matters is the speed with which virtual environments are being introduced in higher education. The pace of technological implementation and development has tended to exceed the strategic planning, institutional policy development, and faculty preparation needed to define these virtual environments as professional workplaces. Clear institutional policies are needed that address faculty concerns about the impact of these on-line environments on their professional lives. (See Chapters One and Two.)

Intellectual access is another barrier to on-line work. On-line teaching and learning require new approaches and skills. These skills and methodologies are still in the development stage. Teaching on-line requires coordination and planning that differs from the lecture or presentation approaches with which many faculty members grew up. Many students in on-line classes also find the process "unnatural" or ill suited to their individual learning styles and needs. Time and training are needed to prepare faculty and students to use these on-line environments effectively, and even more training and time are needed to construct appropriate models for transforming on-line environments into professional communities for teaching and learning.

In spite of the difficulties and problems, many have ventured into the on-line frontier and are discovering or creating a host of new opportunities for professional interaction. They are also realizing that as pioneers they can play a significant role in mapping the landscape of this new environment for other faculty. Their experiences, shared with peers in traditional and electronic formats, are helping inform a growing professional discourse about what virtual professional communities in higher education could be and how we can build them to meet our professional needs.

Building Virtual Communities

On-line groups can feel like community; and on-line environments can help us meet social, instructional, or work related needs while providing data collection and client support opportunities. Most higher education institutions have embraced on-line environments for teaching, learning, and professional development for these reasons and for others associated with pedagogy, competition, and economics.

Choosing to be part of an on-line professional group provides us with increased access to our peers and a way of contributing to a collaborative professional culture. Moreover, on-line professional communities enable us to engage in self-directed or individually guided professional development activities. In these environments we have more choice and fewer constraints on what professional groups we join and what development path we pursue. In effect we get to opt in or out of professional communities because we can visit them wherever they are in the world, stay as long as we want, and leave when we choose. Developing a feeling of professional community with the members of these on-line groups, however, is a different matter. Community building takes time, commitment, and a willingness to work with others in a community way. Community-building in on-line environments is a voluntary and participatory process, but it is also a relatively new and unexplored area of on-line life.

We do not as yet know enough about on-line groups and environments to say that *if you build this, a sense of community will come.* Experiences in virtual environments are like snowflakes—no two are ever alike. Anecdotal reports of people who have made the on-line frontier part of their personal and professional lives do suggest, however, that there are certain things that will increase the likelihood of developing a feeling of community in on-line groups. The most important thing is providing an on-line group with skilled facilitation and democratic leadership.

A sense of community on-line develops in a process of building and rebuilding interpersonal relationships. Let us consider the example of the international group of professionals working together that I posed at the start of this chapter. When an issue or problem arises, as it undoubtedly will in the life of any group, such as a personality conflict, an impending deadline, or a technical problem, one of two things can happen: the group can overcome the problem and move forward, or it can struggle and fall apart. If the relationships that bind a group together on line are not very strong or if there is little commitment or interest in working through problems together, then chances are that we will all go our separate ways and simply do our own thing. If on the other hand our group has a skilled facilitator, a problem can be turned into an opportunity and used as a catalyst to develop a greater sense of closeness and purpose, building a professional community.

On-line group facilitators are called moderators, and they function as group process and discussion leaders. Paulsen (1995) lists the roles of on-line moderator as keeping the group on track, acting as a system manager, adding and mentoring new members, archiving messages, providing administrative support, acting as a mediator, preventing or responding to inappropriate on-line behavior, and generally providing help and encouragement as required by the group's members. Virtual groups without a moderator can still have valuable and informative discussions and interactions; however, the discussions then tend to ebb and flow at the whim of the participants. Consequently, discussions can become disjointed, repetitive, chaotic, or dominated by a few participants, making it difficult to follow a particular topic or line of thought. The experience of being in an unmoderated on-line group reminds me of a large cocktail party where a variety of interesting but often meandering conversations are going on simultaneously. It may be fun, but it may not be productive.

The on-line group environment creates a set of conditions under which group members and moderators must work. Virtual environments for social or professional interaction are predominately text-based structures, and the text base allows for a wide range of social experimentation and communicative interplay. In these environments people use words to define their personalities or personae and to shape their social relationships and work structures. In such environments, without the visual or verbal cues that facilitate face-to-face communication, messages can easily be misinterpreted. One of the dangers in such faceless communication is the phenomenon known as "flaming," which is an excessively emotional or highly aggressive response to someone's message. Flaming can cause a breakdown of on-line group structure. The presence of a facilitative moderator working with an on-line group to build and maintain a community climate is the best way to prevent flaming and one of the major factors in creating successful and sustainable virtual professional communities.

The Relevance of Virtual Community in Higher Education

There is little doubt that the political, economic, and cultural context of higher education in North America is changing rapidly. These changes are also redefining the roles of faculty members within their institutions and within the higher education system. CMC technologies are making it possible to build virtual "town halls" as venues for professional association and development.

In these virtual places geography is neither a limitation on, nor a defining condition of, professional community.

Long-distance collaborations and professional relationships are facilitated in virtual spaces structured to fit our personal and professional needs. As members of these on-line groups, we benefit from diverse perspectives that might not be possible within our own institutions and from opportunities not otherwise available to us. These groups are not communities, however, unless we make them so. Community in virtual environments is something that we must choose and work to create.

Rheingold (1993) said that for the people who inhabit on-line communities the continuing conversations about "artificial intelligence and foreign policy, space shuttles and Star Wars, diatribes, puns, puzzles, gossip, pranks and running jokes became a combination water-cooler and customized daily news medium." On-line environments can feel like communities because of the social relationships that the technology facilitates and that people build together. In higher education the social groups that form in on-line environments for peer support, idea exchange, and collaborative research benefit from an environment that is predisposed to recreate some aspects of community. These groups are largely unaffected by the politics or power relationships of a particular institution. As faculty members we do not generally like to have our institutions evaluate our work, and we certainly do not want to risk appearing uninformed or foolish within our institutions. It is often easier to ask a colleague on-line for help or to question ideas and pose problems for discussion with peers at a distance. On-line communities can feel safer or less threatening than our own institutions.

Critics of higher education claim that institutions do not prepare faculty to use technology in their teaching, research, or professional development. Shanker (1995) and Fullan (1990) suggest that one reason professional development for faculty may be problematic is that administration efforts at "telling" faculty what to do, or how to do it, are not very effective. In fact such administration efforts may backfire, creating a sense of bonding among faculty who see themselves as a group that is increasingly under attack, especially in terms of having technology and technological environments forced on them. Faculty cannot be forced to adopt or use virtual environments, but they cannot ignore them either.

We must realize that only as a community of professionals working together can we create an online environment that will work for us and not against us. There is ample evidence that virtual environments can promote a sense of professional belonging that crosses national and international borders. We need to work together to develop appropriate models of community and skills that will enable us to redefine our professional lives in relation to these new environments.

Marshall McLuhan (1989) rightly suggests that we shape our tools, but then our tools shape us. On-line environments for teaching, learning, and professional development are in the early stages of development and implementation. We must shape these technological environments that offer so much in terms of creating virtual professional communities of professional interest to support our efforts to determine our professional future in higher education. Unfortunately, the pace of technological advance greatly reduces the time available for thoughtful reflection and planning about technology. It took some three hundred years from the time the printing press was invented until textbooks became an integral part of higher education. It has taken less than twenty years for on-line technologies to have a serious impact on higher education.

Conclusion

The time for thoughtful action in higher education is now, and only by working together in collaborative professional communities shaped through dialogue can we make sense of what we are being asked to do with technology. We are called to construct a new professional reality that defines our changing practice. A willingness to enter into a renewed professional community is an important part of shaping this new reality. Community, in face-to-face or virtual settings, is a negotiated, intimate relationship that necessitates commitment and mutual engagement. Interactions in such communities must be based on influence among participants and not on power relationships. On-line professional communities can provide us with a practical and effective model for communicating and working together to define and shape our professional futures in higher education. The first step in creating these professional communities is to address the access and policy issues that act as barriers to full participation by all faculty. Otherwise our on-line professional groups will be just a disjointed collection of privileged faculty individuals who stand little chance of developing a true sense of community.

In this chapter I hope that I have taken a step forward toward articulating a view of community that invites faculty to explore on-line environments for professional association and action and encourages them to shape these environments into neighborhoods of their professional communities.

References

"FIND/SVP." [http://etrg.findsvp.com/pris/pr97/telecomm.html]. 1998.

Fullan, M. G. "Staff Development, Innovation, and Institutional Development." In B. Joyce (ed.), *Changing School Culture Through Staff Development.* Alexandria, Va.: Association for Supervision and Curriculum Development, 1990.

Gozdz, K. "Building Community as a Leadership Discipline." In M. Ray and A. Rinzler (eds.), *The New Paradigm in Business.* New York: Simon & Schuster, 1993.

Hiltz, S. R., and Turoff, M. *The Networked Nation: Human Communication via Computer.* (2nd ed.) Cambridge, Mass.: MIT Press, 1993.

Lieberman, A., and Grolnick, M. "Networks and Reform in American Education." *Teachers College Record,* 1996, 98 (1), 7–45.

McLuhan, M. *The Global Village: Transformations in World Life and Media in the 21st Century.* Oxford, England: Oxford University Press, 1989.

Negroponte, N. *Being Digital*. New York: Knopf, 1995.

Paulsen, M. F. *From Bulletin Boards to Electronic Universities: Distance Education, Computer-Mediated Communication and On-Line Education*. American Center for the Study of Distance Education, Research Monograph, no. 7. University Park: Pennsylvania State University, 1992.

Paulsen, M. F. "Moderating Educational Computer Conferences." In Z. L. Berge and M. P. Collins (eds.), *Computer-Mediated Communication and the On-line Classroom: Distance Learning*, Vol. 3. Skokie, Ill.: Rand McNally, 1995. Available at [http://home.nettskolen.nki.no/~morten/].

Peck, M. S. *The Different Drum*. New York: Simon & Schuster, 1987.

Pinchot, G. "Creating Organizations with Many Leaders." In F. Hesselbein, M. Goldsmith, and R. Beckhard (eds.), *The Leader of the Future*. San Francisco: Jossey-Bass, 1996.

Rheingold, H. *The Virtual Community: Homesteading on the Electronic Frontier*. Reading, Mass.: Addison-Wesley, 1993. Available at [http://www.rheingold.com/vc/].

Senge, P. "The Leader's New Work: Building Learning Organizations." *Sloan Management Review*, Fall 1990, pp. 7–23.

Sergiovanni, T. J. *Building Community in Schools*. San Francisco: Jossey-Bass, 1993.

Shanker, A. "A Reflection on 12 Studies of Education Reform." *Phi Delta Kappan*, 1995, 77 (1), 81–83..

Stone, L. "Feminist Political Theory: Contributions to a Conception of Citizenship." *Theory and Research in Social Education*, 1996, 4 (1), 36–53.

Windschitl, M. "The WWW and Classroom Research: What Path Should We Take?" *Educational Researcher*, 1998, 27 (1), 28–33.

Young, I. *Justice and the Politics of Difference*. Princeton, N.J.: Princeton University Press, 1990.

TONY DI PETTA *is a faculty member in the pre-service department of the Faculty of Education at Brock University, St. Catharines, Ontario, Canada. He is also an on-line forum host for the NODE: Technologies for Learning Network [http://node.on.ca].*

This case study describes our ultimately successful attempts to encourage busy, technology-resistant educators to find time to catch up with current technology.

Overcoming Obstacles Through Use: A Case Study

Karen T. Carey, Shelly M. Dorn

In this chapter we report on the success and importance of technology-assisted small group dynamics and aspects of distance learning in the Joint Doctoral Program in Educational Leadership (JDPEL). This unusual program began in 1991 as a joint venture of the California State University, Fresno, and the University of California. Since its beginning, faculty and staff have concertedly encouraged technology-assisted small group communication among the doctoral students, who need assistance in becoming technologically literate. To do so was not and still is not an easy feat when one considers the fact that the students in this program are older (average age, 47), full-time career educators returning to the university to earn their doctorates. The information provided in this chapter was obtained from exit interviews with graduates of JDPEL, a Program Review Survey, and the experience of working with JDPEL students.

Description of the Program

This joint program was developed to meet an educational need in the San Joaquin Valley of central California. Earning a doctorate while working full time as an educator was virtually impossible prior to its inception. Educators were traveling outside the area to earn their doctorates, and most of the time they did not return to the central region. Therefore, the program was created in an effort to better serve the educational needs of the area.

The knowledge base of any given field should be considered dynamic, rather than stable. Technology enables today's scholars, teachers, and learners to interact in new ways and to keep up with the expanding knowledge base. The scholar practitioners in the JDPEL are individuals who can bring technology tools to their rightful place in the schools of the twenty-first century. As Willis (1997) explained, "Change from the static perspective of knowledge to that of dynamic, ever-changing, and ever-growing cannot come from the technology itself, but from an educational vision, from ideas full of passion and excitement that cross the disciplinary boundaries, drawing knowledge from many sources" (p. 141).

Nontraditional Nature. JDPEL is quite nontraditional. Because of the interdisciplinary, interinstitutional nature of the program it is a "mini-university" within a university. The seven-campus consortium includes California State University, Fresno, and the Universities of California at Davis, Los Angeles, Santa Barbara, Santa Cruz, Riverside, and Berkeley. The main office at California State University, Fresno, provides the support students need in one central location. Professors from each campus teach in the program and serve on the JDPEL Graduate Group. Program administration is handled by California State University, Fresno (Division of Graduate Studies), and University of California, Davis (Division of Education).

The program is interdisciplinary since the faculty are from various disciplines, not exclusively from the field of education. Students choose their specialization focus and the faculty with whom they wish to work. Since 1991, students have chosen to work with professors from such disciplines as Education, Business, Psychology, Science, Criminology, and Music. This flexibility has encouraged a variety of research interests. The students are not traditional full-time students with an on-campus focus. They are part-time students with an off-campus focus and with outside career and family commitments. The educational leadership doctorate offered by JDPEL is for practitioners in the field of education. Each cohort of twelve to fifteen educators forms a cohesive group of colleagues, a model of an effective small group.

Cooperative Effort. All JDPEL course work is completed at California State University, Fresno. The University of California residency requirement is fulfilled by requiring students to register through the University of California, Davis, for one full year while in the program. Professors for the courses are from California State University, Fresno, and from six campuses of the University of California. They either travel to Fresno or participate in courses and committee work via teleconference. Courses are completed in Fresno on weekends since the doctoral students are working full time. The diploma is conferred jointly by the trustees of the California State University and the regents of the University of California. The degree is listed on each student's University of California, Davis, and California State University, Fresno, transcripts.

The rules and regulations of both universities were considered in developing bylaws and guidelines for this unusual, cooperative program. Discussions among the personnel involved at both universities keep the institutions comfortable with day-to-day operations of this "mini-university within a university" program. Since the University of California, Davis, is on the quarter system while California State University, Fresno, is on the semester system credits must be expressed equivalently in both formats before being added to the transcripts of the respective universities. The JDPEL office serves as the navigation system for the various universities and disciplines involved with

JDPEL. Two co-directors supervise the program, one from the University of California, Davis, and the other from California State University, Fresno.

Collegiality. Each group of students newly admitted to JDPEL spends the first one and one-half years as an intact cohort. These groups become quite close and develop unique personalities, structures, and norms similar to those of a family. The students help each other persist and are supportive colleagues. Professors are purposely treated as additional colleagues to the group so that these scholar-practitioners are not moving from an unfamiliar subservient position at the university back to their familiar superordinate position in the public school administrative hierarchy or other leadership position.

Student-Centered. The cohorts are encouraged by staff, faculty, alumni, and fellow students from other cohorts to become teams or families and to mentor each other through the program. Conversations and exit interviews with students indicate that, in many cases, cohort members have become close friends. This type of mentoring is not a goal in itself, but is rather a vital ongoing component of the doctoral program. If the students, staff, or faculty "take a break" from mentoring in this area of technology-assisted small group communication, the program will soon lose some of its unique, nontraditional value. If that happened, the doctoral program could unfortunately take a step toward becoming less student-centered and more traditional (that is, bureaucratic) in nature. At JDPEL peer mentoring and the emphasis on treating all persons involved as colleagues creates an environment similar to the preferred atmosphere of an excellent school setting.

By design the courses are seminars, so that the expertise of the scholar-practitioner students is incorporated into the classes. Classroom theory is clearly linked to practice, and the program is student-centered in all areas including program design and course format.

Peer Mentoring. The most significant impact on learning to use technology results from the peer mentoring aspect of the program. The students not only communicate with each other via electronic mail; they rely on each other to serve as valuable resources regarding what works or does not work in areas such as on-line research and computers in the classroom. The implementation of the technologies as an integral program feature overcomes educational isolation and competitiveness and encourages collaboration and cooperation.

Garafolo and Hansman-Ferguson (1994) stated that such friendships with other students are essential because they "may allow an exchange between equals and may be more accessible to students than faculty mentoring relationships" (p. 95). The themes of student-centeredness and peer mentoring as vital program components are apparent in every aspect of the JDPEL program. MacArthur and others (1995) studied 59 mentors and 154 protégés who participated in "The Computer Mentor Program." They stated, "Key features of the mentoring approach are that assistance is provided within the context of a personal relationship and focused on the individual needs of the protégé. Mentoring programs can break down the isolation characteristic of the teaching profession and encourage collegial interaction and reflection. Mentoring is also one way to provide the school-based collegial support needed to help teachers learn to integrate computers into their instruction" (p. 47).

MacArthur and his colleagues also emphasized the critical importance of administrative support for the success of a technology mentoring program. At JDPEL, it is indeed critical that all students, staff, and faculty are involved in encouraging peer mentoring and group cohesiveness in order to overcome the barriers of distance, full-time work, off-campus focus of the students, and the students' resistance to technology. Technology is a critical factor in the mentoring process.

Continuing Professional Development. Experienced educators encounter a roadblock in catching up with technology because they tend to be isolated in their classrooms or school districts and are otherwise too busy to seek training, mentoring, or help. "User support is a key and costly component of the information technology infrastructure" (Gilbert and Green, 1997, p. 49). Mergendoller (1996) explained that the unique situation of educators affects the nature of this requisite training: "Teachers have become technologically proficient through solitary and school-centered learning. Unlike corporation executives, they can't beep a PC or network manager and ask him or her to stop by to solve a software problem. For teachers, the key trainers are those in the next classroom, not in the district office. Successful teacher development programs integrate professional learning within the regular professional day, take advantage of both informal coaching and structured presentations, and emphasize pedagogy. Technology is seen as a means to an end, rather than as an end unto itself" (p. 45).

The JDPEL experience encourages professional development in two ways: when the students return to their districts, they are able to instruct and encourage others regarding technology, and when they are done with the program, they can continue the network they have established among educational leaders.

Problems Related to Technology

Working full time creates problems for educators trying to attend courses on weekends while catching up with technology. Eventually the tools will indeed save time, so the time spent learning the technology will pay off in the long run. As is the case with many faculty members in coping with today's technologies, however, most of our students also have to be convinced of the value of learning in order for them to use the technology tools. Tools such as e-mail and videoconferencing equipment make it possible for students to reach professors or other colleagues evenings and weekends. Of course a telephone can also serve as such a connection, but the value of e-mail is that individuals can respond at their convenience.

The technology literacy problem is challenging since JDPEL students are successful educational leaders before entering the program. They tend to assume that if they have made it this far relying on low-level technology, they can easily continue to do so. When they begin the specialization phase of the doctoral program, or earlier, they realize that they need the technology to conduct research and to stay connected with faculty and colleagues. This is a difficult time to start "catching up" since it is at specialization that many of the cohort members begin highly individualized research. For the past two years, cohort members have requested an "Internet strategies" specialization course to help with research and e-mail. The course is conducted in a group setting in the computer lab.

Feedback. When the core courses are complete and the specialization phase begins, the students must communicate with professors for independent studies, counsel, and committee work; and they must conduct research effectively and efficiently. At this time, they realize that they need higher-level technology in order to keep up and cannot possibly continue relying on low level technology. The feedback from the JDPEL five-year program review, exit interviews, and conversations with students repeatedly highlights the need for ongoing help with learning technology.

Technophobia. Many experienced educators who refuse to accept computers do so because they do not feel "in control." Aitken (1997) suggested that such technophobes have a point since, "due to the sheer internal complexity, computers too often act in mysterious and unpredictable ways. Even the most experienced users daily find themselves asking 'Why did it do that?'" (p. 180).

According to Baroudi and Levine (1997), people who unreasonably fear technology that could provide benefits on the job or make their lives easier do so because the technology does not meet three criteria of acceptance: familiarity, usefulness, and control. For instance, microwaves, photocopiers, VCRs, and televisions are examples of technology that most consider familiar, useful, and controllable. Therefore, they have no more fear of that particular technology. "Immersing" the JDPEL students in the technology assists in meeting these three criteria. We immerse them by requiring them to communicate via e-mail, research on-line, and use the Internet; become proficient in word processing, database, presentation, and statistical software packages; and take classes and meet with committees via videoconferencing.

Thus they *must* immerse themselves in the technology in order to get course information, conduct research, receive assignments, attend courses, and stay connected with cohort members. Consequently they eventually find the technology familiar, useful, and controllable.

Compelling Need. Every day the compelling need for technological literacy in the workplace is expressed in the news, by government, by industry and business leaders, and by our children's teachers. Researchers such as McGrath (1994), however, noted that the school systems have not entirely adjusted to rapidly developing technological innovations. Sociologists have labeled this phenomenon "cultural lag" (p. 1).

There are difficulties in meeting the compelling need to adopt the new technology. The reality is that educators today are encouraged or often even required to use technology in their classrooms and instructional design. If the faculty lack proper training, however, expensive computers and other advanced technological equipment will be used at the most rudimentary levels. For example, some educators forced to use technology against their will may use a computer, a built-in modem, advanced software, and CD-ROM to teach only the basic components of a business letter. In other words, a *typewriter* would be adequate to replace the expensive equipment. Another problem is that funding often does not follow the promises of politicians who may speak facilely of meeting the technology needs of schools by providing computer labs and Internet connections. As in higher education, many schools and school districts are provided the technology without faculty development programs and good infrastructure support.

Also, educators are simply too busy most of the time to catch up or keep up with technology or even have meaningful meetings or conversation about issues related to technology. People who were previously difficult to reach by phone are now virtually impossible to reach—but one can reach them by conversing via electronic mail. Educators who fear the technology or who refuse to use it may soon find themselves isolated from their peers, subordinates, and students—if they are not already.

Overcoming Technological Illiteracy

Many today consider technology a means of educational reform and improvement, yet Mergendoller (1996) stressed that computer availability does not equate to computer functionality. If the technology is used only to continue standard operating procedures (drill and practice, word processing, reward or play time for the best and brightest in public schools), then the technology tools are just time-saving devices (if even that) rather than innovative educational reform tools. At worst, they increase the division between the haves and have-nots. In order to implement these as tools for educational reforms, both higher-education and K–12 faculty must first be well-trained in the technological possibilities such as: (1) Internet access to worldwide information resources, (2) teleconferencing with professors, researchers, and colleagues, (3) real-time videoconferencing, (4) the use of communication networks, and (5) familiarity with a variety of software programs.

Steps Taken. We have found peer mentoring through the use of technology to be the most valuable tool in encouraging educators to overcome obstacles. The program aspects that encourage the students and the cohorts to form strong networks include (1) providing a program orientation; (2) holding a previous cohort welcoming party for new students; (3) taking the first eight classes as an intact cohort and taking specialization courses in small groups depending on areas of research interest; (4) requiring group projects and papers; (5) holding an annual open house reception, a research symposium, and a graduation reception; (6) founding an alumni chapter; and (7) publishing a biannual newsletter.

Technologies Implemented. The tools of technology-assisted small group communication are e-mail, videoconferencing equipment, computers, software, and the Internet. All this technology may begin to sound expensive. Aitken (1997) pointed out, however, that the technology is getting better while prices are becoming more reasonable. Two byproducts of the Information Age are: (1) greater efficiency and more opportunity than ever to incorporate technology into teaching and (2) the decreasing price of teaching technology. According to (Intel Corporation CEO Gordon) Moore's law, we will see double the performance of the technology at any given price level every twelve to eighteen months. This means that whatever we are using now will be available in a little over a year with doubled power for the same price (Aitken, 1997, p. 72).

The main JDPEL office at California State University, Fresno, provides access to computers and software so that no one has to be left out, no matter what hour they need to do research. For convenience, however, most JDPEL students acquire their own computers, laptops, software, and e-mail access.

E-mail. Courses at JDPEL use e-mail to communicate, and the two most recent cohorts have their own listserv. We now know that students intimidated by face-to-face conversations or by the "expertise" of others involved in a dialogue may become quite prolific using technology-supported communication (Blumenfeld, Marx, Soloway, and Krajcik, 1996). "Students who are shy or who have trouble with English are better able to participate when they have more time to formulate their thoughts and their questions" (Enhagen, 1997, p. 36). According to Baroudi and Levine (1997), the basics of sending and receiving electronic mail can be learned in 15 minutes to one hour.

Siau (1995) argued that electronic communication can be considered superior to face-to-face communication. Although electronic communication does have the advantages discussed above, face-to-face communication allows paraverbal cues to provide feedback, subtle meaning, and other valuable components of communication impossible to transmit over e-mail or fax. The telephone is a little more useful for transmitting paraverbal cues, and videoconferencing is the next best thing to face-to-face communication. "Some have tried to replace the expressive function paraverbal cues by use of emoticons, special symbols and conventions in computer-generated text" (McGrath, 1994, p. 19). Jokes and off-topic communications should not be discouraged because joking and chatting are part of face-to-face discussions, and such exchanges encourage cohesiveness. Professors must, however, keep the appropriate topic in focus while allowing for some peripheral discussion.

Dorn and Papalewis (1997) studied technology advantages for JDPEL students. Most of the 33 respondents in that study agreed or strongly agreed with the advantages of using e-mail listed in the survey: increased productivity, less commuting, reduced stress, flexibility with location, quickly accessible information, flexibility of hours, and access to an enormous amount of information in e-mail correspondence.

At times e-mail and Internet usage are the only ways students can access course information, assignments, or other important information; and they are required to maintain contact. Without this requirement, these busy educators would find it too easy to forget about the technology and do everything the same old inefficient way.

During the second year of operation at JDPEL, we had to stop, as much as reasonably possible, the practice of sending e-mail that was later followed up by a fax, snail mail, and/or a phone call. Before we stopped, many students had simply refused to adapt to the technology or to overcome their personal "cultural lag." Stopping was initially extremely difficult. Students would contact the office, stating that they were not informed of events. Continuous explanations in classes, at program events, among students, and in "The JDPEL News" of the need to use electronic mail eventually spread, however, and we no longer get such telephone calls.

The phrase "as much as reasonably possible" was included above because this is yet another area that requires flexibility and attention to student needs. For instance, a student may be having temporary difficulties with an e-mail account. For this reason, e-mails sent out by the JDPEL office often include the phrase, "let us know that you received this message." Office personnel can then follow up by calling any student who does not respond, guaranteeing that all students receive vital information.

The Internet. E-mail, the Internet, and on-line research offer an abundance of information, but can also present problems (Gleick, 1994). On-line research includes searching the World Wide Web for information, using Web sites designed for educators, searching university library Web sites, and using database systems such as Dialog. "Communication via the Internet is a powerful tool that permits instant dissemination and discussion of the latest educational research. But it is possible to get lost in the waves of information while 'surfing' the Internet" (Pierce, Blomeyer, and Roberts, 1995, p. 26).

One of the few disadvantages of using technology that JDPEL students noted was the tendency to work too much, since modems, fax machines, computers, and videoconferencing equipment make it possible to work from anywhere anytime. Struggling to keep up with the information made available by technology is another commonly voiced disadvantage. One student voiced the common complaint that "It is very easy to get lost in the wonderful possibilities of cyberspace—one is easily sidetracked by intriguing articles and web sites" (Dorn and Papalewis, 1997). The advantage is, of course, that students can find up-to-the-minute resources and quickly communicate their findings with colleagues.

Videoconferencing. Equipment for videoconferencing provides video and audio connections between people at two (or more) separate locations, at a specific time (rather than continuously), usually with a camera at each site. "Videoconferencing has been touted as the prototype for the meeting of the future—a close approximation of face-to-face conditions that would greatly reduce travel costs" (McGrath, 1994, p.14).

JDPEL has its own CODEC (abbreviation for code, decode) two-way audio-video system which is used to conduct courses, committee meetings, and dissertation defenses between California State University, Fresno, and the six consortium campuses of the University of California. Conferences have also included California State University, Sacramento, and the California State University Chancellor's office. JDPEL was one of the first programs to acquire its own videoconferencing system, and at first it was used as a reciprocal service among the various universities involved. Most universities, however, are beginning to charge $50 to $200 per hour for use of their video conference facilities. It is to be hoped that JDPEL will be able to budget for these charges in the future, but the current expense is a challenge since reciprocal usage costs much less. Recently, JDPEL has had to switch to phone conferences for dissertation committee meetings when difficulties arose in attempting to find budgetary support for video conferences. It is distressing to have to regress in technology due to budgeting constraints.

Dealing with Practical Problems

The scholar-practitioner doctoral students at JDPEL value videoconferencing because they can communicate with and learn from professors from remote universities, who otherwise would not have been available. The students, however, have also stressed that the CODEC system is not a reasonable replacement for the physical presence of a professor on an ongoing basis. It is suitable for an occasional lecture or guest speaker as mentioned above but quickly loses value, in their opinions, when it is used for more than three hours of a course. For instance, all the courses at JDPEL are currently conducted on Friday evenings and Saturdays to accommodate those students who are working full time as educators, who must often also commute long distances. When the CODEC is used for two weekends in a row, the students become very tired of the technology. We have found the face-to-face interaction to be a necessary aspect of learning for most of our students.

The professors have noted problems with classroom control in videoconferencing circumstances (yes, even with students with an average age of forty-seven). Students sometimes talk to each other off camera, get up and walk around, or read. We have found it helpful to have a professor at the remote site in the classroom with the students, in addition to the professor on the television.

Having professors at both sites also provides a contingency plan in case the technology breaks down. For example, we had a video conference scheduled for an all-day class one Saturday in April 1998. Due to an unfortunate power outage at the remote site we were unable to use the CODEC. Fortunately the professor at the students' site took over the class, and we heard excellent comments from the students and professors about that class meeting.

We learned from this example to always have a professor at the student site and to also always have the phone number of the remote site so that the professor at a distance can join in via telephone if the technology breaks down. Since JDPEL courses are on weekends, the faculty, staff, and students have had to become fairly proficient with the technology (and adept at implementing contingency plans) because technicians are rarely available on Friday evenings and Saturdays. This experience also provided support for our emphasis on "team teaching." JDPEL strives to be a truly joint program by providing one University of California (Davis, Los Angeles, Santa Barbara, Santa Cruz, Riverside, or Berkeley) professor and one California State University, Fresno, professor for each core course. The staff at JDPEL finds a volunteer from each cohort to be the cohort liaison. The liaison is then responsible for getting the key to a classroom from the JDPEL office before a Friday night or Saturday class, coordinating meetings, and learning to use the CODEC from the JDPEL staff.

Students as Faculty Development Messengers

The benefits of the implementation of cohesive technology-assisted small group communication reach well beyond JDPEL. The lessons shared within this technology-assisted network of professional educators extend to their spheres of influence, to the colleagues, students, and administrators at their places of work. In some cases, doctoral students have been instrumental at their own work sites in developing the technological structure for enhancement of traditional teaching practices. Even the most technology-resistant educators (such as the JDPEL students) may become immersed once they become aware of how software programs and the Internet capture their students' attention.

Implications for Program Faculty

The JDPEL program faculty help students catch up with technology by communicating with them via electronic mail, by providing help with on-line research as necessary, and by participating in courses and committee activities that make use of teleconferencing equipment. Nearly all the faculty have e-mail accounts and use them regularly; this practice was certainly encouraged when the president's office began sending all communications by e-mail. All the faculty are willing to "be on TV" and to serve on dissertation committees that involve faculty from universities hundreds of miles apart.

Staff and faculty of a student-centered program such as JDPEL must be flexible. Student input regarding class scheduling and topics is requested on an ongoing basis. We provide Internet, e-mail, statistical processing, and other software lessons when needed. For example, the "Internet Strategies" course was started three years ago as a specialization course and continues due to student requests for advanced Internet research education.

Implications for Teacher-Administrator Education Programs

Ideally, teachers should be trained in the use of technology in the classroom as part of their teacher education programs (Zachariades and Roberts-Killingsworth, 1995). This capability is an imperative for future teachers. In our experience peer mentoring should also be included as a vital component of such programs.

We are continually learning how to improve the technology and "student-centered" aspects of the JDPEL program. We learn this from discussions and exit interviews with our students. The program is still new, in its seventh year, and we are still working the "bugs" out. We hope that similar programs and teacher-administrator education programs can learn from our successes and improvements along the way.

Blumenfeld, Marx, Soloway, and Krajcik (1996) suggested that more research is needed in the area of technology-assisted small group communication. While an abundance of information and research on small group dynamics exists, technology-assisted small group dynamics is a relatively new area and in need of further study. We plan to continue to examine JDPEL to provide research in this area.

Conclusion

Today people express the concern that technology will replace traditional classrooms. We may have a vision of learners in the near future sitting isolated before their computer terminals, accessing great amounts of information, research, and scholars via computer terminal. Fortunately, most of us require social contact to learn, and we prefer to work with groups. Education is more than just access to information (Gilbert and Green, 1997, p. 49). Our experiences with the CODEC remind us that most students need a certain amount of face-to-face interaction to learn.

In summary, the emphasis at JDPEL is in using technology (1) to enhance (but not replace) traditional pedagogical methods, (2) to save time, (3) to create a model of an effective, successful school setting within the cohorts of scholar-practitioners, (4) to increase networking among scholar-practitioners and faculty, (5) to expand the network of technology-assisted communicating educators, and (6) to share technological knowledge with peers and students at the JDPEL students' places of work.

This chapter, a description of the success we have had at JDPEL in encouraging the use of modern technology tools, has implications for those in higher education struggling to encourage their students or faculty to catch up or keep up through technology. Doctoral programs, teacher education programs, and any other programs working with students who are typically older and have many outside commitments can benefit from incorporating the peer mentoring and immersion strategies outlined in this chapter.

References

Aitken, G. "Music Technology for the 21st Century." In L. Enhagen (ed.), *Technology and Higher Education* . Washington, D.C.: National Education Association, 1997.

Baroudi, C., and Levine, J. "Technophobia." In L. Enhagen (ed.), *Technology and Higher Education.* Washington, D.C.: National Education Association, 1997.

Blumenfeld, P. C., Marx, R. W., Soloway, E., and Krajcik, J., "From Small Group Cooperation to Collaborative Communities." *Journal of Education Researcher,* 1996, 25 (8), 37–40.

Dorn, S., and Papalewis, R. "Telecommuting: Using Technology to Increase Flexibility and Reduce Stress." *Telecommunications in Education News,* 1997, *8* (4), 13–15.

Enhagen, L. (ed.). *Technology and Higher Education.* Washington, D.C.: National Education Association, 1997.

Garafolo, P. L., and Hansman-Ferguson, C. A. "On the Outside Looking In: Women Doctoral Students and Mentoring Relationships." Paper presented at the annual Midwest Research-to-Practice Conference in Adult, Continuing and Community Education, Milwaukee, Wisc., 1994.

Gilbert, S., and Green, K. "Moving Information Technology into the Classroom." In L. Enhagen (ed.), *Technology and Higher Education.* Washington, D.C.: National Education Association, 1997.

Gleick, J. "The Information in the Future: Out of Control." *New York Times Magazine,* May 1, 1994, pp. 54–57.

MacArthur, C. A., Pilato, V., Kercher, M., Peterson, D., Malouf, D., and Jamison, P. "Mentoring: An Approach to Technology Education for Teachers." *Journal of Research on Computing in Education,* 1995, *28* (1), 46–62.

McGrath, J. E., and Hollingshead, A. B. *Groups Interacting with Technology: Ideas, Evidence, Issues and an Agenda.* Thousand Oaks, Calif.: Sage, 1994.

Mergendoller, J. R. "Moving from Technological Possibility to Richer Student Learning: Revitalized Infrastructural and Reconstructed Pedagogy." *Educational Researcher,* 1996, *25* (8), 43–46.

Pierce, J. W., Blomeyer, R., and Roberts, T. M. "Surfing the Internet: A Whale of an Information Source for Educational Researchers." *Educational Researcher,* 1995, *24* (5), 25–26.

Siau, K. L. "Group Creativity and Technology." *Journal of Creative Behavior,* 1995, *29* (3), 43–45.

Willis, E. M. "Technology: Integrated Into, not Added Onto, the Curriculum Experiences in Pre-Service Teacher Education." *Computers in the Schools,* 1997, *13* (1–2), 141–153.

Zachariades, I., and Roberts-Killingsworth, S. "A Collaborative Approach to Helping Teacher Education Faculty Model Technology Helping Integration in their Courses: An Informal Case." *Journal of Technology and Teacher Education,* 1995, *3* (4), 351–357.

KAREN T. CAREY is professor of psychology and co-director of the California State University, Fresno–University of California, Davis, Joint Doctoral Program in Educational Leadership.

SHELLY M. DORN is lecturer and academic coordinator for the California State University, Fresno–University of California, Davis, Joint Doctoral Program in Educational Leadership.

One cannot begin to list all the creative and ever-increasing implementations of new technologies. Each use described is unusual in some way, and each makes use of the technologies for the delivery of faculty development opportunities.

Using Technology in Faculty Development: Practical Examples

Kay Herr Gillespie with Contributors

Remembering ideas of the previous chapters, we now turn to examples illustrating uses of technology for the explicit purpose of faculty development, thereby impacting both faculty life and work. One cannot begin to list all the creative and ever-increasing implementations of the technologies. The following are only a few selected examples—some completed, some in progress, and some still in the planning stage. Each usage described is unusual in some way, and each makes use of the technologies for the delivery of faculty development opportunities. These examples are offered in the belief that they reflect the creativity of many persons and in the hope that they encourage readers' own creativity in new ways.

The standard delivery mechanisms for the substance of faculty development parallel those of regular educational programs—individual consultation, synchronous meetings in a physical location, print and video material. Faculty hold office hours and make appointments with students for individual consultation; faculty developers work individually with faculty members. Students gather for meetings in a physical place; faculty developers offer seminars, workshops, and presentations throughout the academic year at specific times and places. Students use print and video material while faculty developers offer readings and videos. There is nothing wrong with these traditional delivery systems for faculty development activity. However, the examples below invite us to think about doing things differently and perhaps doing different things.

A Corner of Cyberspace for a Statewide Faculty Development Program

This description is provided by PATRICIA KALIVODA, educational program specialist, Office of Instructional Support and Development, The University of Georgia, Athens, Georgia. For more information, contact tkalivod@-arches.uga.edu.

Over the past year at the University of Georgia (UGA) we have incorporated the use of course management software into a year-long, statewide faculty development program. This program is entitled the Governor's Teaching Fellows (GTF) Program. It was established by the Honorable Zell Miller, Governor of the state of Georgia from 1990 to 1998. In the Governor's vision, the program would address the pressing need of faculty members from both public and private institutions to use new instructional technologies. Selected competitively and reimbursed for their efforts, the Fellows come to the University of Georgia for two weeks in the summer and then six times for three days during the academic year. During this time they engage in instructional development activities and design and implement an instructional project. UGA's Office of Instructional Support and Development and Institute of Higher Education co-coordinate the GTF Program. Now in its fourth year, the program has brought together 106 faculty members from thirty-seven institutions in the State of Georgia.

Beginning with the 1997–98 program year, we introduced the use of WebCT, course management software. This software provides a means of cordoning off a corner of cyberspace for the exclusive use of students—faculty in this instance; entry to the course is password protected. While there are several such software packages (Schmitt, 1998), UGA elected to license WebCT, which stands for Web Course Tools. Dr. Murray W. Goldberg at the University of British Columbia developed it to facilitate the creation of sophisticated World Wide Web-based educational environments. It can be used to create entire on-line courses or to publish materials that supplement existing courses. Aside from facilitating the organization of course material on the Web, WebCT also provides tools and features that can be added to a course. Examples include a conferencing system, on-line chat, student progress tracking, group project organization, self-evaluation, grade maintenance and distribution, access control, navigation tools, e-mail, timed quizzes, automatic index generation, and course content searches ("World Wide Web Course Tools," 1998). WebCT helps faculty members develop sophisticated Web-based courses without their having to become computer programmers. Though designed for managing an instructional course, we are trying WebCT as a tool for enhancing a faculty development program. Currently the GTF WebCT faculty development course has seven categories: GTF brochure, current fellows, communications, GTF presentations, symposia information, links to resources, and alumni GTF projects.

We have identified five objectives for using a WebCT "course" with the GTF program. The first is to have participants experience what it is like to be students in a WebCT environment. Many are new to the practice of using Web pages in their instruction. Moreover, most have little or no experience with Web-based course management software. We believe it is difficult to imagine the possibilities of this instructional technology without having first practiced navigating the software. Our hypothesis is that an authentic experience with such software enhances the comfort level with the technology prior to using it in one's course.

Our second objective is to allow participants to stay "connected" within and across cohorts. In campus-based faculty development programs, one of the frequently recognized positive outcomes is the chance to interact with peers from other disciplines. In the GTF Program, participants meet faculty not only from other disciplines but also from other kinds of institutions. With this technology we can keep participants *connected within a cohort* and *across* cohorts over space and time.

The electronic communication features "built in" to WebCT—chat room, bulletin board, and private e-mail—allow us to extend the impact beyond the physical meetings of the group(s). Community is created and collaboration is encouraged, both of which are significant factors in the process of effective faculty development. To date, these communication tools are activated just for the current group of Governor's Fellows.

The third objective in using WebCT is to provide materials to the participants in an appropriate manner under the educational fair use of copyrighted works guidelines. Understanding that this is an ever-changing gray area in the law, we are currently working under the assumption that posting copyrighted materials within the confines of the course falls under the educational fair-use umbrella when working in a password protected Web environment.

In accord with the program requirement of completion of a project, the fourth objective is to provide an opportunity for collaboration on group projects from the home campuses. The WebCT Student Presentation Tool allows participants to place material onto the WebCT server which other participants can then access. It can be used to have students (the faculty) create multimedia WWW presentations on particular topics. The intent is to have the Fellows from institutions across the state work on group projects and then present the projects to the whole group when they come to the Athens campus.

Our fifth and most basic goal for the use of WebCT in the GTF Program is to provide logistical information to the participants including links to maps, to symposia agendas, to various higher education-related Web resources, and to various university and community-activity Web pages.

We have used the chat room several times. For example, at the close of one symposium we took a field trip to Atlanta to meet Governor Miller. The next week we designated two times when the chat room would be "open" for discussing reactions to this meeting. To date, we have used the presentation feature once for a PowerPoint presentation on teaching and course portfolios. The co-coordinator of the GTF Program uploaded a PowerPoint presentation for the co-presenter of the session, a Governor's Fellow from Abraham Baldwin Agricultural College, to review and edit in preparation for the forthcoming meeting of the entire group.

Utilizing the "course" in the administration of the faculty development program has a number of advantages; but at the same time it presents several challenges, frustrations, and disadvantages. The biggest drawback is that participants must "log into" the "course." If they do not do so daily, they may miss important logistical messages on the bulletin board. In this respect, using the participant's home campus e-mail address is more effective than posting to the WebCT bulletin board because most of the participants check their campus e-mail more frequently than they log into the WebCT course. This is an important lesson: participants learn firsthand what their students might experience if they do not log into the WebCT course daily.

A second disadvantage is that not all of the participants' institutions use WebCT, which is just one of many Web-based course management software packages available. Thus, not all of them are equally enthusiastic about having to learn navigation of this particular environment. Our rationale for encouraging the participants to experience WebCT is that the opportunities and pitfalls in using Web-based course management software are probably generalizable across the common software providers.

A third disadvantage and frustration in using WebCT as a faculty development tool is the infinite amount of time that the course manager (instructor and faculty developer in this instance) can spend on managing the course. The learning curve for a "non-techie" administrator is steep. Course management requires daily attention. Moreover, developing Web pages for inclusion in the course, uploading materials, overseeing the bulletin board and private e-mail are all time-intensive activities.

In summary, use of the technological capabilities in this instance represents an enhancement of this statewide faculty development effort, and we consider the experiment worth continuing. Participants gain insights into the pedagogical opportunities and challenges of course management software, and the faculty developer benefits from managing the course. Our future goals for this faculty development WebCT course are to include all current and former Governor's Fellows and a needs assessment instrument under the WebCT quiz tool and also to make the course the primary means of communicating with the Fellows, thereby immersing them in the WebCT environment.

Moving On Line to Teach On-Line Teaching

This description is provided by SALLY L. KUHLENSCHMIDT, director, Center for Teaching and Learning, Western Kentucky University. For more information, visit the course Web site at [http://edtech.tph.wku.edu/~internet/], or contact sally.kuhlenschmidt@wku.edu.

Most faculty members learned to teach from personal classroom experience. They may be unaware of the knowledge base on effective instruction and thus unlikely to seek development opportunities. Many, however, are interested in learning the new technologies, and now the communication tools allow faculty to study and "meet" conveniently. At Western Kentucky State we are finding that an on-line course covering issues in Internet-based instruction satisfies faculty needs and interests.

The two-credit-hour graduate course, "Issues in Using the Internet in Instruction," is conducted primarily via the Internet and is graded pass/fail. The target audience is faculty and administrators. The course is offered for credit for several reasons. One objective is for faculty to fully experience the world of the Internet student, including the entire course structure and pressures of evaluation. A second reason is that students find time management of an Internet course a challenge. Using the traditional structure with a grade encourages participants to prioritize course activities and commit to the process. Finally, offering the course for credit was a means of "paying" for instructor development time. It is a graduate level course because of the complexity and integrative nature of the information presented.

On completion participants can (1) design a course or modify administrative policies for Internet instruction, (2) understand principles of instruction adapted to the Internet, (3) increase personal comfort with using technology, (4) understand how technology will affect higher education, and (5) reflect on the experience of being an Internet student. As a prerequisite, participants are expected to have posted a Web page, assuring a common language and set of skills. About one half of the spring 1998 participants were beginners, posting their pages in time for the class. Of course, e-mail and Internet access are required.

The course focuses on issues which are likely to endure and influence education whatever the specific technology, not on the details of technology. Other course topics include new teaching options, ethical and legal dimensions, implications for assessment of learning and faculty work, and changes in scholarship.

Several 1998 participants reported instructional improvement in face-to-face courses. Two participants reported decreasing lecture time and increasing classroom activities. Several wrote course objectives for the first time or identified activities, technological and otherwise, that they could use in their face-to-face courses.

The course is structured around weekly readings and supplemental lessons posted at the class Web site. Readings include text chapters, quick reviews of numerous Web sites, and on-line articles such as an Internet instructor's reports about teaching on-line. Activities include partnered tasks, visiting Web courses, and making decisions about constructing an Internet course.

Interaction is critical for learning and is conducted via Web-based discussion groups. Participants can post or read comments at any time. I also provide several general Web discussion areas, our "student lounge." In the last third of the semester we use a listserv for discussion, and we also visit a Multi-User Dungeon to experience on-line chat. Phone, fax, and snail mail are all used in the course although e-mail is used most for individual conversations. Six of the 1998 participants attended an optional face-to-face meeting about halfway through the semester, and I was also able to take six participants to a nearby conference on technology.

I ask participants for a written commitment to two regular course site visits per week, and spring 1998 participants reported averaging about four hours weekly doing course activities. My role as the instructor and faculty developer is to facilitate participants' efforts. I monitor participant activity, encourage participant interaction, and contact those from whom I have not recently heard. Periodically I visit participant Web sites to provide reaction to their postings. During the course participants are making foundational decisions for their Internet courses, solving problems such as potential copyright violations, and learning about various forms of interaction. All are expected to contribute weekly to discussion.

The course was advertised in the teaching newsletter, but the primary means of obtaining students was personal contacts with faculty. After this initial experience, the course will be more aggressively marketed, though enrollment will be limited. Thirteen faculty participated the first semester. I also asked a colleague from another school (110 miles away) to participate in the role of mentor.

This course also encouraged institutional change. As it moved through the course approval process, I answered committee questions about the implications of Internet instruction. Several administrative units had to adapt their procedures to this new course. Our initial experience with this faculty development on-line course has been positive, and it offers a model for learning by doing—using the technologies to learn the technologies.

Improving Teaching and Learning Through Web-Based Feedback

> This description is provided by ANITA GANDOLFO, director, Center for Teaching Excellence, and LIEUTENANT COLONEL CHARLES G. POWELL, United States Military Academy. The views and opinions expressed herein are solely those of the author and do not represent the official view of the U.S. Military Academy, the U.S. Army, or any other agency of the U.S. government. For more information, contact za4643@exmail.usma.army.mil.

The Center for Teaching Excellence at the U.S. Military Academy at West Point is charged with general faculty development as well as the integration of technology in instruction. West Point has a ubiquitous computing environment, a robust infrastructure, and an institutional vision for the use of technology for instruction.

Since all faculty members and individual cadets have desktop computers, our intranet offers rich opportunities for the instructional use of technology. While we are engaged in the development of course Web pages and customized multimedia programs, we are also using technology to enhance the classroom learning environment by providing instructors with tools that create a more collaborative relationship with their students. On our Center's Web page we offer three feedback systems for faculty members to use with their students.

Like many institutions, we collect feedback from our students at the end of every semester in every course, but this data is fully formative in both plan and operation. That is, cadet feedback is not used for evaluation of teaching, but to increase the instructors' awareness of student perceptions of their teaching. Only the instructor receives data on an individual class. The course directors of multi-section courses and department heads do receive aggregate information.

The end-of-course system began as a standard feedback instrument, and it has evolved so that individual departments, course directors, and instructors have their own customizable subsections and can write questions in whatever format they wish. The Web-based electronic system began as a cadet design project in computer science and was further refined by one member of the design team as an independent study project. During the development process it became clear that some additional distinct tools were needed, and the faculty advisor developed them. These other two tools fill important niches in the feedback process between faculty member and student.

While the end-of-course feedback system is formative in intent, such an instrument has limited usefulness for the students themselves. In addition, it is our feeling that instructors need more frequent feedback from students in order to learn and develop as teachers. For some time we had encouraged faculty members to do interim course feedback of their own design, but many were reluctant for a variety of reasons.

We addressed faculty concerns about time and student anonymity by developing an electronic, Web-based process that provides instructors with a simple, user-friendly, flexible means for obtaining anonymous student feedback. Instructors using this system testify to its value; and the number of instructors regularly using it is increasing.

Based on the same principles of learning and using a similar system, we next decided to address a critical learning issue. Today's college student does not always arrive with a high level of academic sophistication. In fact, research indicates that most high school students are unfamiliar with independent studying and rarely do homework. This is a nationwide problem and poses a particular problem for us because our cadets do not have the luxury of wasting the years of their West Point experience. They literally must "hit the ground running" when it comes to study and homework. We wanted to develop a system that would help the instructor guide learning by monitoring cadet class preparation, and we used Angelo and Cross's (1993) classroom assessment techniques (CATs). CAT principles and the system enable instructors to assess cadets' preparation before class, so they can modify instruction to address any specific learning problems.

In addition, they can choose specific CATs to help students deal with a particular assignment. For example, suppose an English professor has assigned a nonfiction essay to be read and wants to focus on the essay's theme. The "one-word journal" CAT assignment on the Web asks the student to choose one word that encapsulates the essay theme and to explain the word choice in no more than 100 words. When the professor arrives at work the next morning, the computer will deliver the students' anonymous journal entries for review. Our system currently offers twelve CATs from which faculty members can select, but the number can be easily expanded to meet the needs of any particular instructor.

Since these tools were designed by cadets and a full-time faculty member on his own time, expensive or difficult computer systems or software were not used. A premium was placed on developing robust, functional software that could easily be ported between Windows NT or Unix Web servers. The development tools had to be either freely available or very cheap. For the Academy to adopt the system, it was also critical that it could be sustained by having "code" that was largely self-documenting and easy to maintain. All the Web scripting was done using Perl, which is freely available and runs a variety of operating systems and Web servers. Students and instructors have had little trouble understanding the operation of the feedback tools.

An added benefit is the move to a more "paperless" office. At the Academy level, there was a significant saving in the costs of materials—survey and mark-sense forms—and personnel hours.

We know from discussions with our faculty members that our electronic feedback systems, while technically simple, offer a rich new resource for improving student and faculty learning.

The Web as a Resource for Faculty Development

This description is provided by REBECCA S. MORE, administrative director of The Harriet W. Sheridan Center for Teaching and Learning at Brown University. For more information, visit the Web site at [http://www.Sheridan-Center.stg.brown.edu], or contact Sheridan_Center@Brown.edu.

The Harriet W. Sheridan Center for Teaching and Learning, Brown University, was established in 1987 to support faculty in the development of their teaching performance. The Center offers resources to both graduate teaching assistants and faculty members. The Sheridan Center is committed to the concept of teaching and learning as a partnership between faculty member and student, which supports the open curriculum concept at Brown.

In 1997, as part of its tenth anniversary celebration, the Sheridan Center collaborated with Brown's Scholarly Technology Group to develop a Web site to enhance the delivery of resources to Brown faculty and TAs. The goals of the Web site are to provide busy faculty with easy access to Center services and to promote reflective teaching practice through the medium of interactive computer technology.

Sheridan Center programs, services, and publications are designed to complement each other in supporting reflective teaching practice. A case in point is the range of resources offered for faculty to explore the effectiveness of their "Syllabus Construction." Available Center resources include a short seminar on Syllabus Construction, an Individual Course Consultation service, a Teaching Handbook (both in printed and electronic form), and an electronic "workshop."

The Web site has provided the ideal forum for making the issues of "Syllabus Construction" available. Author Michael Woolcock together with Roger Blumberg and David Reville of the Scholarly Technology Group adapted the *Constructing a Syllabus* handbook electronically and also developed the electronically delivered "Syllabus Construction Workshop." The "workshop" provides a chance for Brown faculty to examine four syllabi, one from each of the major academic divisions, and to revise their own syllabus right on the site. Each syllabus is accompanied by a series of questions designed to prompt the reader to reflect on the clarity of the course goals and objectives. Other questions address the range of objectives (quantitative and qualitative) or the degree to which the measures of student assessment are consistent with the goals and objectives of the course. Through examination of the syllabi of colleagues from other disciplines, it becomes easier for faculty to imagine what students comprehend when looking at their own syllabus. The revised syllabus may then be sent electronically through the "Course Publisher" link to the Computing and Information Services Division for conversion into a Web site. The technology of the Web site was designed to assist faculty to reflect on how course structure shapes educational outcomes and the role of an effective syllabus in maximizing student learning.

The Center and the Scholarly Technology Group have designed an interactive "Variation in Learning workshop" where faculty can experience their own diverse learning styles and reflect on how accessible their courses are to diverse student learning styles.

Distanced SGIDs

This description is provided by ART CRAWLEY, director, Center for Faculty Development, Louisiana State University, Baton Rouge, Louisiana. For more information, contact acrawle@lsu.edu, or visit the DISD Web page at [http://www.disd.lsu.edu].

The Division of Instructional Support and Development (DISD) at Louisiana State University at Baton Rouge supports teaching and learning by providing integrated services and resources through its Center for Faculty Development, Center for Instructional Technology, and the Measurement and Evaluation Center.

In 1995, responsibility for the University's distance learning initiatives was vested in the DISD, working with the Division of Continuing Education. Less than a year later, a statewide compressed video network was established, connecting five of the University's campuses: Baton Rouge, New Orleans, Shreveport, Eunice, and Alexandria. In 1997, DISD was awarded a three-year state grant from the Louisiana Department of Natural Resources Energy Efficiency and Conservation Program entitled "Utilizing Compressed Video Technology to Save Energy." The objective was to demonstrate the energy-saving potential of interactive, two-way video and audio delivery of educational resources via compressed video to sites in Louisiana.

With the grant, ten LSU faculty are selected each academic year to receive a $1000 salary stipend and a $1000 grant for the development of course materials. The funds can be used for Web-based or on-line course development; the development of presentation software and graphics; and the purchase of commercial software, instructional videos, and CD-ROMs for use over the compressed video network. The grant includes provision for training and necessary support to translate traditional classroom teaching strategies to the distance learning setting. A team of DISD professional staff including an instructional designer, a faculty developer, an evaluation specialist, and an instructional technologist are available to work with these faculty in groups and individually.

As an assessment component within the instructional design process each faculty member is required to meet three times during the semester with the faculty development director and to produce a course portfolio (Cerbin, 1994). The course portfolio consists of a teaching statement or philosophy, a learner-centered syllabus, analyses of student learning outcomes and student feedback, and a course summary, which includes an instructor self-assessment and course evaluation.

Using new technologies, a Small Group Instructional Diagnosis (SGID) is used to obtain student feedback on each distance education course receiving grant support. Each site has received the Student Feedback Form ahead of time for distribution by a proctor. This form asks students to reach consensus on three questions: (1) What do you like about the course? (2) What areas need improvement in this course? and (3) What suggestions do you have for implementing the needed improvements? The sites are engaged in the small group process simultaneously through the compressed video system, and the instructor from the home site is not present. The facilitator instructs the class at the remote site to form groups of four to six members. After group consensus has been achieved, which takes approximately fifteen minutes, the facilitator contacts each site and a site spokesperson discusses the responses, a process which generally takes another fifteen minutes. The remote responses are then collected via fax and summarized for use in consultation with the instructor. To date, seven instructors have engaged in the SGID process with over two hundred fifty students participating at six different remote sites. Responses have also helped the project directors to make changes in faculty training as well as pedagogical and equipment modifications within the compressed video network.

The Electronic Salon

This description is provided by KAY HERR GILLESPIE, editor and faculty consultant, Office of Instructional Support and Development, The University of Georgia, and professor emerita, Colorado State University. For more information, contact kaygi2@aol.com.

During the fall of 1994 an electronic faculty discussion group was conducted at Colorado State University as a faculty development event presented by the Office of Instructional Services. The spirit was that of an "electronic salon," providing opportunity for discussion of a subject perceived to be of a somewhat intellectual and rarified nature. Since the formalization of faculty development at Colorado State in the early 1970s, there had developed a comprehensive array of programs, services, and activities addressing issues of teaching and learning effectiveness for both faculty and graduate teaching assistants as well as efforts relating to advising, faculty research, service and outreach, administrative development, and personal needs.

To address the intellectual dimension of faculty interests and needs, traditional discussion groups were routinely included in programming and generally focused on a particularly significant book. Such groups are not an uncommon feature of faculty development programs. Generally, however, only a small number of persons are able to participate, and numbers usually dwindle as the term nears its end. For this reason, this electronic salon was presented using a listserv. The hope was to increase access and participation and also to proffer a subtle and invitational introduction to the pedagogical possibilities of the listserv. When this event occurred in 1994, faculty in general were only beginning to become aware of and make use of the potential of e-mail, listservs, and, to a lesser extent, Internet capabilities for instructional purposes.

The substance of the salon was the work of the famed myth scholar Joseph Campbell and provided opportunity to examine some basic beliefs and assumptions. The well-known, eight-part PBS videotape discussions between Campbell and Bill Moyers on *The Power of Myth* provided the point of departure. Participants watched one video per week (the videos could be accessed in several ways). The faculty developer facilitated the weekly discussion, which built on each preceding week. Among the surprisingly large number of fifty-seven persons enrolled were not only faculty but also administrators, extension personnel, and staff. The message traffic was intense and at times exhilarating. Indeed, the only problem was finding the time to reflect and respond with the depth one wished to have. At the close of the event, an on-campus face-to-face meeting was held to provide a sense of closure.

Evaluations assessed not only the success of the event but also participants' reactions to engaging in this kind of technologically facilitated discussion. Some expressed frustration at not being able to "see" others. One respondent commented, "I found the medium of discussion to be better than I originally expected. I have been a user of e-mail for quite a while, but this was my first experience in this sort of usage. It lent itself well to the discussion, and I would like to consider further areas of discussion." Another said, "This was an interesting experience and more thought provoking than the usual colloquium." A third wrote, "Heavens, yes! Let us talk about things to each other. It is a good sanity check from time to time."

This program was very successful in the number of persons enrolling, probably first and foremost because of the somewhat unusual subject for a faculty discussion group. The possibility of participating by electronic technology in such an event without time- and place-bound meetings, however, clearly enabled more persons to participate than is generally the case for such groups. We were able to build an expanded kind of intellectual community, which introduced faculty members to the pedagogical possibilities of electronic communication. The event was subsequently also offered to alumni in cooperation with the Alumni Association of the University, and it was likewise successful and well received.

The experience of an electronic salon is recommended to others for consideration as an opportunity to create a new kind of intellectually connected and cross-disciplinary community within an institution. We have very quickly become far more widely accustomed to e-mail and list discussions, and with the use of Web technologies such an event could now be presented in an even more technologically sophisticated manner than was originally the case.

Electronic Mentoring: An Idea for This Time?

> This description is provided by BOBBI NICHOLSON, Leadership Studies, Graduate School of Education and Professional Development, Marshall University. For more information, contact bnicholson@mugc.edu.

While the value of formalized mentoring is increasingly recognized, most institutions still lack the ongoing commitment of resources necessary to provide the level of guidance junior faculty seek. The College of Education and Human Services at Marshall University is attempting to remedy that situation through the use of technology and the valued services of faculty *emeriti*. While our proposal remains in the discussion stage and formal action has not yet been taken by the dean, it has been approved by a faculty committee.

Current research reports that the mentored protégé indicates greater job satisfaction and smoother professional socialization than would likely be possible without a planned mentoring process. There is even a suggestion of a positive correlation with publication and grant productivity (Blackburn, Chapman, and Cameron, 1981; Cameron and Blackburn, 1981; Chao, Walz, and Gardner, 1992; Diehl and Simpson, 1989; Luna and Cullen, 1995). Luna and Cullen (1995) also mention enhancement of the organizational culture, a sense of continuity about the institution and its people, heightened competency and productivity, the optimization of human potential and resources, and the attraction and retention of good faculty. One problem identified is the lack of available mentors.

There is, however, a pool of available competent talent who have the experience, the wisdom, and perhaps also the time to serve as mentors: the *emeriti*. Their skill levels and knowledge are no different the day after they retire from the day before. They remain competent, well-informed, and familiar with the institution's social and political cultures. Professionally mature, they bring a tradition of inquiry as well as a wealth of valuable experience to support the protégé in search of new ways to conceptualize teaching and learning. In addition, they also have the professional connections to create or promote career advancement opportunities for the protégé. Although faculty *emeriti* often leave the institutional community, use of the new technologies can overcome geographical separation.

These technologies are well suited to facilitating the mentor-protégé relationship. Most institutions are already investing heavily in technology, and increasingly persons maintain their own computer systems at home. Thus, creative opportunities for developing effective mentoring programs could flourish with the establishment of fundamental policies and practices such as extending *emeriti* perquisites and offering them training.

Our College plan, simplified, is to use the existing campus network. Technical support could be provided by graduate students, interns in computer services, or even proficient faculty themselves. While a list of available professors *emeriti* has been compiled, none besides the two involved in the development of the proposal has been contacted, since the plan is not yet approved. A list of junior faculty, defined for this project as those at the instructor and assistant professor ranks, has been obtained.

The lack of a mentoring program squanders talent and is an absence that will be more keenly felt as institutions of higher education try to meet the increasing enrollments predicted over the next decade (Jones, 1997). A thriving mentoring program implemented through the innovative use of electronic technologies can harness both the proven talent of the *emeriti* and the potential talent of their protégés in a mutually beneficial relationship that also advances the interests of the institution.

References

Angelo, T. A., and Cross, K. P. *Classroom Assessment Techniques: A Handbook for College Teachers.* (2nd ed.) San Francisco: Jossey-Bass, 1993.

Blackburn, R., Chapman, D., and Cameron, S. "Cloning in Academe: Mentorship and Academic Careers." *Research in Higher Education,* 1981, *15* (4), 315–327.

Boyle, P., and Boice, B. "Systematic Mentoring for New Faculty Teachers and Graduate Teaching Assistants." *Innovative Higher Education,* 1998, *22* (3), 157–180.

Cameron, S., and Blackburn, R. "Sponsorship and Academic Career Success." *Journal of Higher Education,* 1981, *52* (4), 369–377.

Cerbin, W. "The Course Portfolio as a Tool for Continuous Improvement of Teaching and Learning." *Journal on Excellence in College Teaching,* 1994, *5* (1), 95–105.

Chao, G., Walz, P., and Gardner, P. "Formal and Informal Mentorships: A Comparison of Mentoring Functions and Contrast with Nonmentored Counterparts." *Personnel Psychology,* 1992, *45* (3), 619–636.

Diehl, P., and Simpson, R. "Investing in Junior Faculty: The Teaching Improvement Program." *Innovative Higher Education,* 1989, *13* (1), 147–157.

Jones, R. "The Kids Are Coming." *American School Board Journal,* Apr. 1997, pp. 21–24.

Luna, G., and Cullen, D. *Empowering the Faculty: Mentoring Redirected and Renewed.* Washington, D.C.: The George Washington University, 1995.

Schmitt, J. "WWW Course Management Software—Lists." Towson State University. [http://saber.towson.edu/~schmitt/courseware/coursew.html]. Jan. 20, 1998.

"World Wide Web Course Tools." Additional information is available from the University of British Columbia WebCT Server (the developers of WebCT). [http:// homebrew. cs.ubc.ca/Webct/]. June 3, 1998.

KAY HERR GILLESPIE is editor and faculty consultant in the Office of Instructional Support and Development at the University of Georgia in Athens, Georgia. She is also professor emerita at Colorado State University.

INDEX

Back Issue/Subscription Order Form

Copy or detach and send to:
Jossey-Bass Inc., Publishers, 350 Sansome Street, San Francisco CA 94104-1342

Call or fax toll free!
Phone 888-378-2537 6AM-5PM PST; Fax 800-605-2665

Back issues: Please send me the following issues at $23 each
(Important: please include series initials and issue number, such as TL90)

1. TL _____

_____

_____

$ _____ Total for single issues

$ _____ Shipping charges (for single issues *only;* subscriptions are exempt
from shipping charges): Up to $30, add $5^{50} • $30^{01}–$50, add $6^{50}
$50^{01}–$75, add $7^{50} • $75^{01}–$100, add $9 • $100^{01}–$150, add $10
Over $150, call for shipping charge

Subscriptions   Please ❑ start   ❑ renew my subscription to *New Directions
for Teaching and Learning* for the year 19___ at the following
rate:

❑ Individual $56   ❑ Institutional $99

NOTE: Subscriptions are quarterly, and are for the calendar year only.
Subscriptions begin with the spring issue of the year indicated above.
For shipping outside the U.S., please add $25.

$ _____ Total single issues and subscriptions (CA, IN, NJ, NY and DC
residents, add sales tax for single issues. NY and DC residents must
include shipping charges when calculating sales tax. NY and Canadian
residents only, add sales tax for subscriptions)

❑ Payment enclosed (U.S. check or money order only)

❑ VISA, MC, AmEx, Discover Card #_____ Exp. date_____

Signature _____ Day phone _____

❑ Bill me (U.S. institutional orders only. Purchase order required.)

Purchase order #_____

Name _____

Address _____

_____

_____

Phone_____ E-mail _____

For more information about Jossey-Bass Publishers, visit our Web site at:
www.josseybass.com   **PRIORITY CODE = ND1**

UNITED STATES POSTAL SERVICE™

Statement of Ownership, Management, and Circulation
(Required by 39 USC 3685)

1. Publication Title	2. Publication Number	3. Filing Date
NEW DIRECTIONS FOR TEACHING & LEARNING	0 2 7 1 _ 0 6 3 3	10/14/98

4. Issue Frequency	5. Number of Issues Published Annually	6. Annual Subscription Price
QUARTERLY	4	$56 – indiv. $99 – instit.

7. Complete Mailing Address of Known Office of Publication *(Not printer) (Street, city, county, state, and ZIP+4)*

350 SANSOME STREET
SAN FRANCISCO, CA   94104
(SAN FRANCISCO COUNTY)

Contact Person
ROGER HUNT
Telephone
415 782 3232

8. Complete Mailing Address of Headquarters or General Business Office of Publisher *(Not printer)*

SAME AS ABOVE

9. Full Names and Complete Mailing Addresses of Publisher, Editor, and Managing Editor *(Do not leave blank)*

Publisher *(Name and complete mailing address)*

JOSSEY-BASS INC., PUBLISHERS
(ABOVE ADDRESS)

Editor *(Name and complete mailing address)* MARILLA D. SVINICKI
CTR FOR TEACHING EFFECTIVENESS/UNIV OF TX AT AUSTIN
MAIN 2200
AUSTIN, TX   78712-1111

Managing Editor *(Name and complete mailing address)*

NONE

10. Owner *(Do not leave blank. If the publication is owned by a corporation, give the name and address of the corporation immediately followed by the names and addresses of all stockholders owning or holding 1 percent or more of the total amount of stock. If not owned by a corporation, give the names and addresses of the individual owners. If owned by a partnership or other unincorporated firm, give its name and address as well as those of each individual owner. If the publication is published by a nonprofit organization, give its name and address.)*

Full Name	Complete Mailing Address
SIMON & SCHUSTER	P.O. BOX 1172
	ENGLEWOOD CLIFFS, NJ 07632-1172

11. Known Bondholders, Mortgagees, and Other Security Holders Owning or Holding 1 Percent or More of Total Amount of Bonds, Mortgages, or Other Securities. If none, check box ▶ ☐ None

Full Name	Complete Mailing Address
SAME AS ABOVE	SAME AS ABOVE

12. Tax Status *(For completion by nonprofit organizations authorized to mail at special rates) (Check one)*
The purpose, function, and nonprofit status of this organization and the exempt status for federal income tax purposes:
☐ Has Not Changed During Preceding 12 Months
☐ Has Changed During Preceding 12 Months *(Publisher must submit explanation of change with this statement)*

PS Form **3526**, September 1995   *(See Instructions on Reverse)*

---

13. Publication Title	14. Issue Date for Circulation Data Below
NEW DIRECTIONS FOR TEACHING & LEARNING	SUMMER 1998

15.	Extent and Nature of Circulation	Average No. Copies Each Issue During Preceding 12 Months	Actual No. Copies of Single Issue Published Nearest to Filing Date
a.	Total Number of Copies *(Net press run)*	1881	1983
b. Paid and/or Requested Circulation	(1) Sales Through Dealers and Carriers, Street Vendors, and Counter Sales *(Not mailed)*	440	113
	(2) Paid or Requested Mail Subscriptions *(Include advertiser's proof copies and exchange copies)*	832	845
c.	Total Paid and/or Requested Circulation *(Sum of 15b(1) and 15b(2))* ▶	1272	958
d.	Free Distribution by Mail *(Samples, complimentary, and other free)*	0	0
e.	Free Distribution Outside the Mail *(Carriers or other means)*	176	131
f.	Total Free Distribution *(Sum of 15d and 15e)* ▶	176	131
g.	Total Distribution *(Sum of 15c and 15f)* ▶	1448	1089
h. Copies not Distributed	(1) Office Use, Leftovers, Spoiled	433	894
	(2) Returns from News Agents	0	0
i.	Total *(Sum of 15g, 15h(1), and 15h(2))* ▶	1881	1983
	Percent Paid and/or Requested Circulation *(15c / 15g x 100)*	88%	88%

16. Publication of Statement of Ownership
☒ Publication required. Will be printed in the WINTER 1998 issue of this publication.
☐ Publication not required.

17. Signature and Title of Editor, Publisher, Business Manager, or Owner

SUSAN E. LEWIS
DIRECTOR OF PERIODICALS

Date 10/14/98

I certify that all information furnished on this form is true and complete. I understand that anyone who furnishes false or misleading information on this form or who omits material or information requested on the form may be subject to criminal sanctions (including fines and imprisonment) and/or civil sanctions (including multiple damages and civil penalties).

Instructions to Publishers

1. Complete and file one copy of this form with your postmaster annually on or before October 1. Keep a copy of the completed form for your records.

2. In cases where the stockholder or security holder is a trustee, include in items 10 and 11 the name of the person or corporation for whom the trustee is acting. Also include the names and addresses of individuals who are stockholders who own or hold 1 percent or more of the total amount of bonds, mortgages, or other securities of the publishing corporation. In item 11, if none, check the box. Use blank sheets if more space is required.

3. Be sure to furnish all circulation information called for in item 15. Free circulation must be shown in items 15d, e, and f.

4. If the publication had second-class authorization as a general or requester publication, this Statement of Ownership, Management, and Circulation must be published; it must be printed in any issue in October or, if the publication is not published during October, the first issue printed after October.

5. In item 16, indicate the date of the issue in which this Statement of Ownership will be published.

6. Item 17 must be signed.

Failure to file or publish a statement of ownership may lead to suspension of second-class authorization.

PS Form **3526**, September 1995 *(Reverse)*